Sketches from Paraguaná

Venezuela

Ina Whitlock

Also by the Author:

Eating the Chinese Pear
travelogue-memoir

Of Love and Loss
poetry

Copyright © 2011 by Ina Whitlock

Published in the United States by
Spirit Journey Books, Vashon Island, Washington
iwhitlock@centurytel.net

ISBN: 978-0-910303-65-1

Printed in the United States of America

Edited by Eagle Eye Proofreading & Editing
Book design by Sy Novak

Paraguaná Peninsula
Los Taques
Amuay
Judibana
Las Piedras
La Vela
Caja de Agua
Carirubana
Punto Fijo
Punta Cardón
Cerro Santa Ana
Golfete de Coro
Coro
Map illustration based on
Pescadores de Paraguaná
by M. M. Suárez and E. B. Gómez

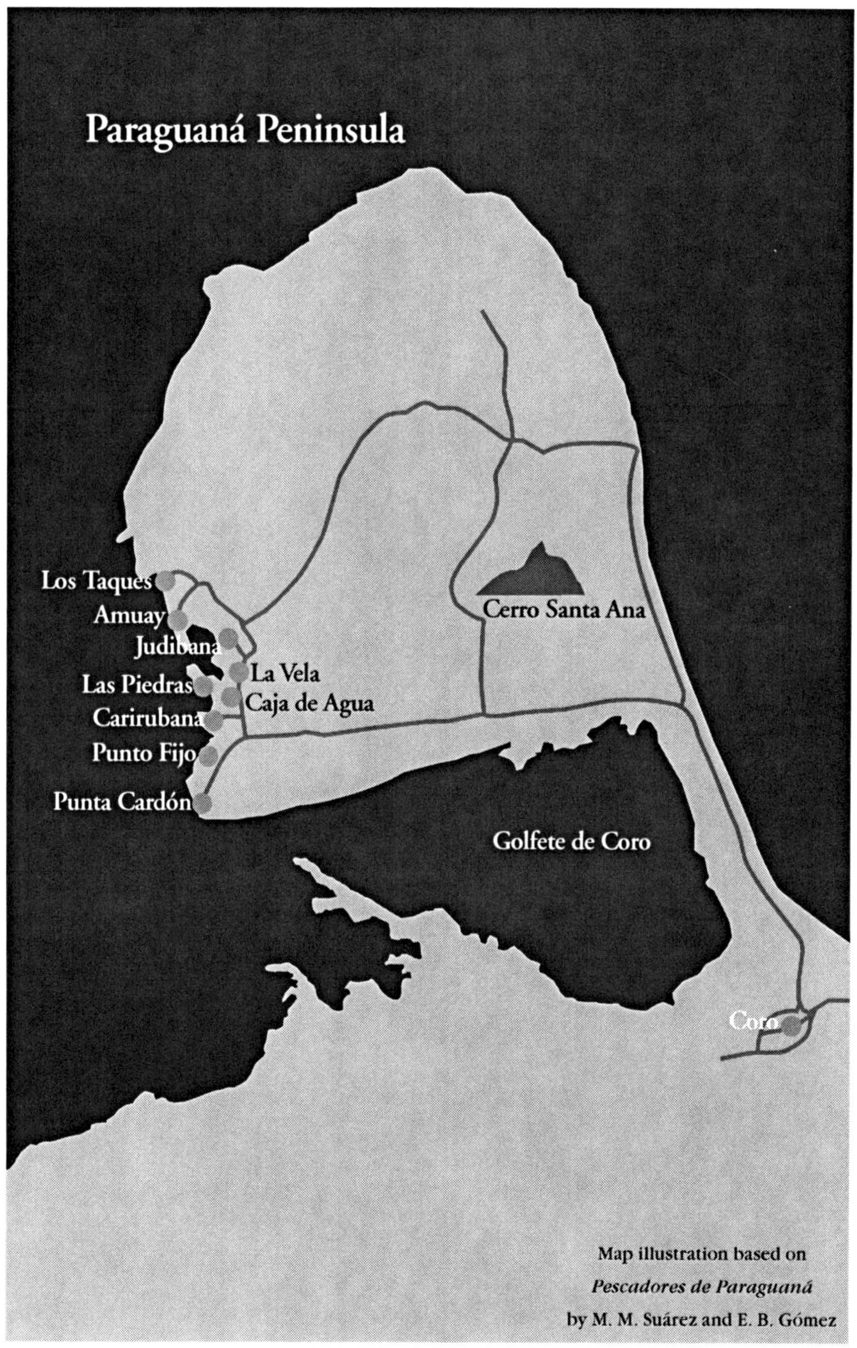

i

"Place never really stops informing us, for it is forever astir, alive, changing, reflecting, like the mind of man itself. One place comprehended can make us understand other places better."

~ Eudora Welty

Author's Note

Half a century ago I lived on the Peninsula of Paraguaná, where the largest oil refinery in the world was situated. I lived there as an *extranjera*, a foreigner, with my husband and children in a Quonset hut on Amuay Bay. Later we resided in company housing in the newly formed community of Judibana, created to serve workers of Creole Petroleum Corporation.

With artist friends I often went to the fishing village of Las Piedras to paint and draw. On what I thought would be my last day (though I returned twice more to live in Venezuela), I drove to the village alone, trying to hold all that I could in memory. I longed for words to express what I had seen and felt for the land and its people.

Much has changed since then in worldviews: technology, economics, politics, demographics, and awareness of fossil fuel and global climate change.

All situations and characters in these stories, these *cuentos*, are fictional—some drawn from life, some sketched from memory and imagination, others taken from newspaper articles of the day.

DEDICATION

To my husband, John Moore Whitlock—my greatest support, who made this book possible and to whom I owe so much. He came to Paraguaná as a young man and returned some years later as manager of the refinery. He also negotiated in the nationalization of Petróleos de Venezuela.

To Mary Bard Jensen, who first gave me the confidence to write the stories, and to those on Vashon who patiently listened as I read. To Joyce Delbridge and the Night Writers and the Memoir Class; to Patricia Lourinda Looker, who started the process of publishing this manuscript; to Michael O'Donnell for his technical expertise; and David Hinchman of Vashon Print and Design for his assistance. To Nancy Morgan, Eagle Eye Proofreading & Editing, for editing and publication support, and Novak Creative, Inc. for design and layout.

My special thanks to La Rita Smith for her drawings. And deep appreciation to Ivonne Escobar de Kommer for her insights; Beverly Winge for her long-standing encouragement and comments; and for the helpful suggestions of readers Shelly Whitlock and C. Hunter Davis.

To the people of Paraguaná, who inspired me to write and were so generous in shaping my life. My gratitude and abiding love to La Rita Smith and Margaret De La Cour Pinedo, my painting pals those many years ago.

ILLUSTRATIONS

Covers: NASA Space Photograph
ERTS Satellite of the Paraguaná Peninsula

Drawings by permission of La Rita Smith:

The Patio

Group of Village Boys

with instruments

Single portraits of boys

All other drawings are by the author.

Contents

Paraguaná

The sun rises quickly, ascending in a great arc over the Mar Caribe and the sprinkled chain of islands that stretch from Florida to the coast of Venezuela: to the north, lighting islands' verdancy, and to the south, transforming in golden glow those lands arid and blown by trade winds.

At the end of that chain of islands, the peninsula of Paraguaná lifts its head over the body of Venezuela like an old man bending to the West, away from the sun and hot breath of wind and sifting sands. The face of the peninsula is pocked by coral rock, covered with a stubble growth of cactus and scarred at the chin by a highway that converges in a system of pipes, a freckling of oil tanks, and stacks of an oil refinery that has changed the face of all Venezuela.

Calle Zamuro

The sun flashes against oil tanks, brushing across sand flats, striking white against the cupola of a small church in the fishing village of Las Piedras. Rays spill over full leafing flamboyant trees, breaking into myriad bright splashes that dance with wind-flickering shadows and fall at the feet of an old man.

Pedro's parched face is laced in light and shade. He comes to the village plaza each morning to sit under the trees, his frayed straw hat on his lap. He listens to the younger men as they congregate. On passing, they pat him on the shoulder. *"Viejo, como estas hoy*? Old man, how are you today?"

His immutable companion, the bust of El General Simón Bolívar, most courageous, most revered father of Venezuelan independence, "Libertador de la Patria," faces Calle Zamuro, the street by the plaza.

In a sudden scurrying of dust, Pedro hears boys shout as they chase a squealing sow. *"Vaya, tonta.* Go! Go!"

Vultures, startled from a repast crushed on the road, flap in wide circles and settle on a tile rooftop. A hand clasps Pedro on the shoulder.

Salvatore, a fisherman of the village, tells Pedro of his visit to Padre Ignacio this morning. Soon would be the time for the annual celebration of Saint Carmen and the blessing of the fishing boats at the start of the fishing season. Pedro himself took part in the celebration years past, when the statue of Saint Carmen, patron saint of fishermen, was carried from the church to the boats and then across the bay to all the fishing villages, boats from each community joining the others in a grand procession on the sea.

Now the ceremony proceeds from a dock near the oil refinery. Padre Ignacio blesses the boats and with full sail, flares shooting into the sky, the statue of Saint Carmen leads the fishermen to the church in Las Piedras.

As Salvatore disappears through the arched doors, Pedro thinks of the crucifix of the suffering Jesus with blood streaming from his hands, and how the narrow windows guard the cool interior from blinding light and strange happenings that rise like dust on Calle Zamuro, the street of the vulture.

SALVATORE

A great blazing disk, the sun slipped ever nearer the gold-dipped edge of the sea. Salvatore, the fisherman, turned toward the shore, eyes steady from long years peering over a sun-swept sea. He sat aft, leaning back, his left arm over the tiller, muscular shoulders relaxed. A breeze ruffled his shirt, his pants ragged at the knee. With a bare foot he tucked his straw hat, grey with age, wide brim rolled up, under the seat.

The sun would drop below the sea as the boat passed the outer sandbar. When he and his two companions reached the village, it would be night and unloading fish in the dark was bad, more so when the boat ought to be rigged for an early start tomorrow.

They were late this morning. They had run up the coast to the fishing beds from the small settlement of Los Taques that was protected from trade winds by coral cliffs. Tonight the boat would pass the *pueblo*, going on to Punto Fijo, where the market for fish was better because it was closer to the refinery and local restaurants that cater to foreigners.

His boat, the *Pajaro*, was some hundred meters from shore. Salvatore looked back on cliffs red in reflection of the sinking sun. Los Taques was disappearing, but he still could see the small square of his hut among the others and bait fishnets hung to dry over sticks in the sand.

Several figures moved along the beach. Was one Evito? That boy of his never stopped running! And where were the others? Ana ought to be cooking supper now. Poor Ana! How thin she appeared this morning, how dark under her eyes when she rose before the sun to make his coffee and pack *arepa,* corn cake, in his tin. She was a good woman. Never questioned. Took what she was given. He couldn't complain of her, like others. When she was young, how wild she had been, wild and changing as the sea. But that was long ago. Now she was like a lantern, the wick burning low, flickering once in a while, the brightness gone.

Ana had given him eight children. The first five, boys. He thought with satisfaction that that was right for a man like himself. His oldest son would soon be coming with them on the boat, as Salvatore had gone with his own father from the time he was twelve. They had made a record catch that year, his first. It had been a good year for all the boats.

Salvatore thought again of what had been on their minds today. Perhaps that was why he and his companions were slow in returning tonight. How long could his boat run with any profit against the new boats that the foreigners were bringing here? Would his men agree to a full week of fishing? The price of fish was going down. They would have to agree.

"Hey, I ask you, Salvatore," one of the fishermen forward of the engine pit shouted, "what right have those foreigners to come here and take our business? They will push us out of the sea with their big boats and fishing nets. Why doesn't the government do something? Keep them out? We are the true *paisanos*, the countrymen, aren't we? What right have they?"

"I don't know. I don't like this any better than you. We will have to start earlier in the morning. We didn't have a bad catch today, did we?"

"But with a few sweeps of their big nets they catch more in a few hours than we get all day. I don't like it! Taking our fish from us!"

Salvatore stood up as the boat rounded the sandbar. He braced the tiller with his left calf, moving the boat deftly out of the protective leeward bay, around the point of the great sandbar and on toward the village. He scanned the water for the white frothing of rocks below. The boat took one swell that slung salty droplets on his face and lips. He laughed, wiping his face with his arm. The boat headed into a trough, was lifted upward, then dropped again. These, he thought, were the best moments of the day, obeying the sea, free of the involvements of land, the demands of women and children and money, always money.

The sun fell below dark water. Salvatore and the others lounged quietly. The motor throbbed and they slipped into a nether world of contemplations and undulating satisfactions as the boat plunged into the cool breath of night. For a while Salvatore gazed at the stars. Then a few lights of Punto Fijo took their place, blending on the horizon with stars above.

Salvatore was anxious to reach shore. The *Pajaro* had not come here for several days. When they arrived, would he see a light burning in the window of his hut? It was late, later than usual. Would his little Salvatore be sleeping? And Carmencita? How he hoped Carmen would be there in the doorway, awaiting him, her young eyes bright.

The Gift of Ice

A highway passes the refinery and a lake of eleven million barrels of fuel oil, then descends over ochre cliffs to vast sand reaches and a sea that embraces the fishing village of Las Piedras. There seems little to connect the rows of tanks in the refinery and the rows of huts in the village other than the highway itself, yet they are intertwined as nebulously as the shifting sands on which they are built.

Past windblown mesquite trees stands a chapel. Enclosed within low walls are crosses of the village dead, visages as in life, leaning one upon another; some tended, some unloved, others forgotten—fancily wrought iron crosses, a few brightly tiled, others two sticks bound together, long weathered, some marked by rusty tin flowers.

The highway passes salt flats where old women bend low to gather salt for fish and boys play *beisbol.* Beyond, seen against a cerulean sky, is the cupola of the church.

In the village, a fisherman slaps a *carite* down in front of his hut. Soon his wife comes and carries the fish inside. A boy calls at the door. "Mama! I see the painters coming!"

"Good! Then you will stay from under my feet this morning. And, I pray, you will keep away from the icebox! I have precious little ice and the electricity does not come until this afternoon. Go, my son, and see if the truck comes bringing water."

"*Si*, Mama!" The boy runs down the road. Yes, he is sure he sees the water truck. It brings water from a reservoir far away.

Foreigners brought water to the desert to supply an oil refinery that was built in that desolate place because of the location, as a port for oil tankers and to support a national guard so that the government might protect itself from insurrectionists, bandits, and smugglers—occupations that rivaled those of goat herding and fishing. The refinery brought the National Guard and water and electricity to the desert. Each day five million gallons of water flowed through a pipe from a reservoir in the mountains across seventy miles of barren land. As if by magic, water spigots appeared on a few corners. People had water for drinking and washing. But miracles run dry and a few years later, there was no more than a trickle of water, for no one had maintained the water system. Today a truck comes down the highway bringing water.

Just as water had come to the village with the building of the refinery, so also the village received electricity. The oil company installed an electrical system and the people had light by night and a few had electric iceboxes. But no one ordered replacements or maintained the generator. Now there is no electricity, except when a truck comes. Then the village has electricity for two hours.

~~~

A car bounces along flat sand that forms a roadway by the shore, then stops. Two North American women get out of a station wagon, instructing several young children to remain inside, to play with crayons and paper and to drink fruit juice. The women settle themselves on stools to sketch the huts, to paint boats bobbing in the water, and to draw the faces of the village children who gather about them. One of the women asks if there is water nearby for her paints. A boy runs to his hut. "Mama! The American wants water for her paints!"

"Then run next door to Carmen, perhaps she has water."
~~~

Soon the boy comes with a jar of water for the painter. She paints and her brush splashes water over white paper and onto the sand. Village children watch curiously.

Boys pose, hands on hips, brown chests expanding, grins on handsome faces as the other woman draws them. Then her hand moves in pen strokes that make a long thick braid. "Look! She draws Marina!"

"See over there, that one is painting the church." The artist dips her brush into green, then red, then blue, as villagers partake in the excitement of seeing white paper become filled with color.

A fisherman glances from the paper up to the church tower. Yes, she paints well. It was almost equal to their fine church with the cross on the tower that thrusts majestically into the sky. To the crowd he says, "I'd like to see her paint a red snapper, or maybe an eel. A dogfish, now that's a pretty sight!"

From the foreigner's station wagon a small voice shouts, "Mama! I want to get out! I'm hot! I'm hungry!"

"Drink your juice!" calls the American. A few boys and girls of the village peer through half-opened windows of the car, trying to talk with the little foreigners.

When the sun is directly overhead, the painters pack their stools and paints and paper into the station wagon. A child screams. A small hand is caught in a car door. The American rushes to assure herself that the accident is not serious and clutches the child to her. The child wails. A voice says, "Señora, come to my house. I have ice for the child's hand."

The American follows the woman of the village to the door of her hut. The woman takes the remaining piece of ice from her icebox. A pink crease shows across the small palm.

"With ice the hand will be better. *Pobrecita*, poor little one," she says, "it gives her pain. Here, *niñita*, is ice for your hand."

While the painter holds the child, the villager ministers to her and the crying ceases. "Señora, you must watch that the discoloration does not remain on the child's hand."

The two women's eyes meet for a moment and the ice that the villager presses against the small hand melts, falling in droplets.

As she turns to leave, the American says, "Many thanks."

"*De nada*, Señora. It was nothing."

And indeed, the American does not think again of that gift of a piece of ice.

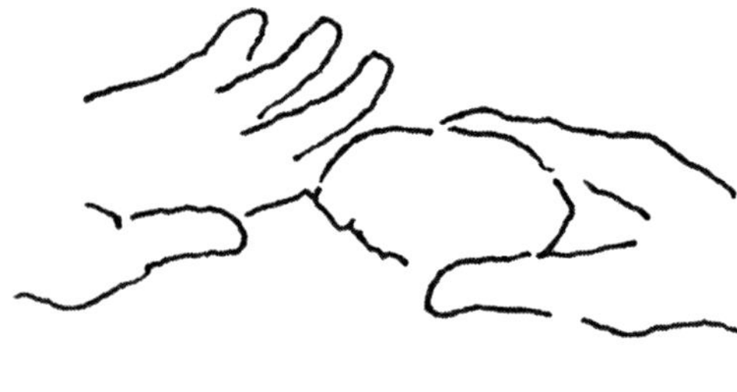

Red Interior

Night invades the village with an oppressive silence as voices hush and light grows dim. The thrust of life from past to future is suspended. But on Calle Zamuro, from the house of Rosita, the little seamstress, the smoldering glow from a lantern reflects red interior walls and filters through a barred window onto the street. Rosita turns from her treadle sewing machine.

"Federico!" She waits for a moment, then calls again, "Federico! Won't you answer me? Do you ever listen to your poor mother? No!"

"Eh?"

"Federico! Oh, were you sleeping, son?"

Federico stands tall in the doorway, shirt rumpled, eyes half opened.

"Why do you not answer when I call?"

"Eh, Mama? You call me?"

"If I call once, I call a million times! And you do not answer."

"Eh?"

"And if you say something to your poor mother it is 'eh'! Why are you not kind to your mother?"

Federico shifts his feet in the doorway.

"My son, I want to talk with you."

"About what?"

"That woman!"

"Who?"

"You know who I mean. The woman."

Federico shrugs his shoulders. "I have many friends."

"But, I pray to God, not many who are women of the street!"

"She is not…"

"Then it is so! I knew it!"

"Eh?"

"You know well what I mean – that – woman! And, my son, the sorrow of my life, do you know, every day some kind neighbor comes and throws me tidbits, like a poor defenseless bird in a cage, hints of your escapades. And it is I who must bear the humiliation, I, your poor mother who must bear the guilt for you and go to the church each day to pray for your soul. *¡Ay!* Is it fate that sent me such a son?"

"Fate, little mother? I thought it was a sailor, a sailor named Fred."

"My dear sorrow, listen to me! Don't be foolish. Don't close the door on luck when it comes knocking. You have opportunity handed to you and you do not take it. Can you not see? Can you see nothing at all?"

"Eh, little mother? You say let's have a talk and I can't make any sense of it."

"Federico! How can you talk so to your mother? The one who raised you, worked night and day to feed you and care for you since the day you were born? Yes, I worked until my fingers ached and my eyes burned through my head, here at my sewing machine, always working for others, never for myself! Always for you, everything for you, my son, all these years. And now I have the right to be proud of you! It is a mother's right. Do you understand?"

"So you must go to church and pray for me?"

"The villagers come to me with stories about you and all the time I am praying to God that they are not true—all those lies! Federico, I'm telling you, you have a real chance to better yourself! To marry well, into a good family. That Esperanza's family does not object to you, for that you should offer thanks!"

"But Mama!"

"But no! Listen to me. For once do what is sensible. Accept Esperanza. She is crazy for you!"

"Yes, crazy is the word."

"With love for you. A girl of fine qualities who will be faithful to you."

"A lump of butter. Not to my taste."

"And what is your taste? That woman?"

"I care nothing for Esperanza."

"There are other things to consider, my son."

"Yes, her father's store. She has all the virtues of her father's store—the pots, the pans, the knives."

"She is single-minded in her devotion to you."

"Yes, simple-minded."

"She is worthy of your affection."

"If ever I marry it will be to have sons, not a job in Papa's store."

"And how will you marry without a job?"

"I get by."

"Yes, singing at the hotel once in a while. How many times have I told you that if you would get a job at the refinery…"

"But I have tried, Mama. They only want mechanics, and I am no mechanic."

"So what are you then? A fool who will throw away chances to better himself."

"Mama!"

"Federico, my son, if you have thought for nothing else, at least give thought to your little mother. I can only tell you what is good for you. I cannot make you listen. But someday, when your hot blood has cooled, you will regret. Regret that you did not take your mother's advice and marry Esperanza!"

"Federico? You are not going out at this hour? To that woman? Are you listening to me?"

But already he had slipped through the door and onto Calle Zamuro.

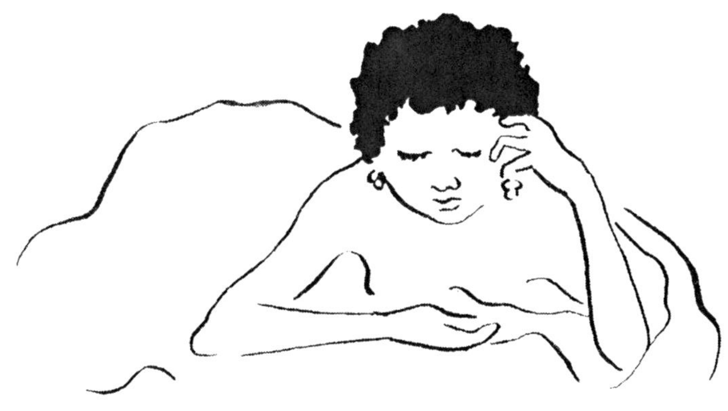

LELA

Lela walked into the sun on a cloudless morning of life, a child breathing freshness through her whole being. She emerged from under green leaves of banana trees, sipping liquid innocence, drunken with the possibility that someday her hands might hold riches as golden as the sun.

From Aunt Juana's hut on the mountainside Lela looked to the pueblo below. She skipped down the warm path to the Iscardo store, pails swinging from her hands, singing *"Leche para mi tia, leche para comida!* Milk for Aunt Juana, milk for lunch!"

She walked past the house with Spanish grillwork at the windows. That was the finest house in the pueblo, but even then, the house was crumbling at the edges, walls cracking in layers of ochre plaster. Next was the hut of the good Señora Villaba, who knew how to read and write and held classes for those in the pueblo who wanted to learn. But Lela did not like school much and stayed only until she could read picture magazines that older girls sometimes brought back from the big town far down the mountain. The magazines were filled with movie stars, the latest fashions, scandals, and stories with titles like "24 Hours in the Life of a Model" or "We are the Girls of the Show." Lela liked those.

She passed the plaza where the little church stood, the only building in the pueblo painted white. She had walked into Señor Iscardo's store many times as a child—but that day, how old was she? Ten, eleven?

Sometimes Lela came to the store for salt fish, rice, or a dried leaf of tobacco or goat cheese and sometimes for a stalk of cane sugar to suck. Occasionally she came for milk, if the "money was thick." Tinned meat and the lumps of candy that Sr. Iscardo bought "special" were too expensive. The store had few other foodstuffs to sell.

Sr. Iscardo saw the milk pails she carried. "So your Tia Juana has extra change, no?"

He sauntered to a dark room at the back of the store and returned with a large covered bucket dripping from the stream water that kept it cool. "Some cream too?"

"No, just milk. Aunt Juana can't afford to feed us all on cream."

Sr. Iscardo raised the container and poured the yellow cream from the top into a pitcher. "Shame a pretty girl like you can't enjoy good things. Drink a little of the cream of life. Sometimes it sours one, not getting much. So, how many *bolivars* do you have?"

"I can give you only two. Tia wants a handful of black beans also."

When she was small, Sr. Iscardo would set her on the counter and let her play with the bell-shaped weights of his scale while he gathered her purchases. Aunt Juana had often warned her. "Watch that Sr. Iscardo does not put his finger on the scale!"

He took two handfuls of black beans and weighed them. "Well, Lela, what more do you want today?"

She tucked the package of beans into a tight cord at her waist that Aunt Juana made her wear to keep *"la forma."* Sr. Iscardo looked at her. "Nothing left for a piece of candy?"

Lela shook her head.

"That's too bad. A pretty girl like you!" He went to the small glass case where he kept special treats. "Take one, have a piece of candy!"

Lela always glanced into the case, choosing the piece she would have if she had a few *centavos.*

"Take one," Sr. Iscardo said again.

She had kept her eyes off the case until that moment, but Sr. Iscardo reached inside, withdrawing a piece of sugary coconut. He held the candy to her. She shook her head no, but she could smell the sweetness. He smiled at her. "No, Lela, go on, take it! It doesn't cost anything."

She smiled at him then, happy to have her wish come true. She took the oh-so-sweet stringy candy into her mouth, pushing it around with her tongue, savoring it in a kind of ecstasy.

"Remember, Lela, how I used to set you up on the counter when you were a little girl?" He put his hands on her waist and drew her to him as if to lift her up.

She remembered Aunt Juana's warning, "It is bad, now, to let the men touch you!" Lela pulled away, grabbed the milk pails, and fled from the store.

She turned back once and saw Sr. Iscardo standing in front of the store, hands on his hips, laughing.

Banana leaves hung over the steep path to Aunt Juana's hut and Lela tried to keep them from the milk. It took all her effort to carry the pails. The weight of the handles bit into her palms. She heard a rustling behind her, thinking the sound was a wild pig. Then dark shapes appeared in the shadows of the leaves. Dogs! A pack of wild dogs was chasing her, barking at her.

"Don't let them get the milk," she cried to herself, "don't let them get the milk!" On she ran, struggling up the steep path, pulling the buckets as high as she could to keep the dogs away, but they rushed at her—growling savagely, jumping, clawing her. Flames licked at her legs and thighs. She stumbled, milk splashing, flashes of blue pain hiding the path.

At last, she made the clearing and flung herself through the door of the hut, sobbing, calling breathlessly for Aunt Juana, but no one answered. Only then did she realize that the dogs were gone, that she must have dropped a pail, for she carried only one. The packet of beans was still tight at her waist, but what would Aunt Juana say? Milk had splashed over her torn dress, and down her legs blood-red ribbons burned.

~~~

"*¡Ay!*" Was it true? Lacquered fingertips threw back the coverlet. Yes! There were the crinkled scars across her thigh.

The rude brightness of morning entered through a broken shutter into the hotel room, and the trumpeting of a record player and "El Gallo De Oro," the golden cock. Lela wrapped the coverlet around her, dancing to the window where sounds of the street mingled with the music: cars honking, babies crying, and two angry women in front of the New Store shouting at each other. The store sold U.S. made ovens, Japanese radios, and Italian fans and typewriters.

Small shops opened to the street, merchandise spilling onto the busy thoroughfare. Woven hammocks striped blue, red, and yellow hung from shop walls. Trinkets caught her eye. Plastic balls with clown heads that bounced back if she punched them, gaudy yard goods sold in the shop of the Arab ("*Importadas, Señorita!*"). Huge crepe paper *piñatas* dangled from ceilings in the shapes of birds and boats. A woman splashed a bucket of water onto the narrow walkway. Lela laughed at the impossibility of washing away the dirt. Even white confirmation veils under glass cases yellowed from dust that rose on the street.

Lela searched for her clothes. Dressing, she put on her one pair of shoes. The heels needed repair, but did she have enough money in her purse? Never enough! Ah, yes! Federico had left bolivars.

Lela clutched her purse tightly as she walked down the dark corridor and into the sun. She went to find Gonzalez, to buy a ticket on the 5 y 6. She would find him on a corner waving slips and shouting, "Win today!"

And if she were lucky, she would win! She might even find
~~~

Federico.

Lela passed the shops, hips swinging, her favorite music – "Tres Caballeros" – soaring blatantly, unrestrained onto Calle Del Futuro.

SEASCAPE

Waters of the Caribbean in shifting colors of ultramarine and viridian curl toward a narrow beach. Here the coastline of Paraguaná alternates in stretches of sand and headlands of coral rock that double back, forming small coves and larger bays. Black smoke from a gas flare trails across the sky to the west and at sea a tanker moves from the horizon toward the refinery dock.

Two men walk over a crest of sand. One holds a small child. The infant stares wide-eyed at the sea that at mid-morning seems a wild immensity struggling to engulf the shore. Awe sweeps over the men, surging through their consciousness, then subsides in formless unknowns. The men sigh deeply and walk on.

At the shoreline the sea licks hungrily in iridescent scallops where sandpipers run, their motion discernable only in delicate forked imprints soon washed away.

"How fast they go!"

"Listen, Segundo, I'd not run on the ground if I could fly!" says Eduardo.

"Unless you had a car."

"If I had a car, man, you wouldn't catch me here, I would be in

Caracas." Eduardo unfastens a thermos from his belt and stretches out in the shade of a lean-to. "Segundo, set Reina here."

Fingers of the wind rustle the palm frond siding. Segundo's moustache brushes the child's cheek as he stands her in the sand. A thin dress puffs over her slight frame. Her legs support her for a moment, then she sits down abruptly. Free from the encircling arms of her father, she hears the sea tumbling toward her and shrieks.

"Poor little one! She is afraid." Waves break, bubbling onto the sand. "Do not have fear, Reina de las Rosas. The sea will not get you, though it swallows poor children, sometimes."

Eduardo chucks her tiny chin. "Queen of the Roses, do not be frightened. Do you not know that today is your first birthday and now you have reigned one year in the house of your papa?"

Reina looks up at Eduardo with eyes so black they show no white, and so large they overshine the glow of her pale copper skin. Ringlets of black hair curl toward small gold earrings fastened in her delicate earlobes. A gold crucifix at her neck catches the sun, and on her wrist an amulet, the red and black seed of the *aojadura*, protects her from the Evil Eye.

"See there, Reina, the sea is not angry but gently rolls toward the shore."

"Ah, but Eduardo, the sea is a woman who beguiles us to set sail, and in moods of calm or rage draws us to her heaving bosom!"

"But, I don't love the sea so much that it could be a woman! *El Mar* it is!"

"And terrifying, sometimes!"

"Ay, out there, a man doesn't have a chance if his luck is bad."

"When were the boys lost?"

"A year ago."

"All in the village stood on cliffs above the sea, watching, waiting for news of the lost boys. You remember, Eduardo?"

"I do not forget. First the dory was sighted far out. Then wind blew hard to the west and the boys were carried into the sunset."

"Salvatore took the *Pajaro* out, hoping to find them."

"But all he brought back was the dory."

"And woe to the village."

"We waited until we saw nothing but stars."

"And waited the next day, gazing out to sea." Segundo sighs. "The third day, only the mothers yet stood vigil on the cliffs. And the *tiburones*, the sharks, had a feast."

"No one can be sure of the sea, Segundo."

"It is the great unknown before all of us. Like entering into partnership with a woman, you are never sure. I don't have to tell you, Eduardo. Why, just today, my wife said to me, 'Segundo, take Reina to the shore to bathe her, then you will not be bothered while I am busy arranging the house for the birthday celebration tonight.' That is what my wife said to me, but do you know what in truth she meant? She wished the opportunity to search the house for the money I have hidden. Five hundred bolivars. That is all that remains from the days when I worked for the construction company, before I got a job at the refinery and got a company house."

"It has been some time now."

"Do you remember, Eduardo, how it was before the refinery was built? The village was small then, a few people, no cars, no airport— just lots of goats and fish and cactus."

"Twenty years ago I was a babe!"

"Yes, a babe in long pants! Think how it is, Eduardo, and then be sorry for your old friend. I have come here to wait while my wife finds the money, so that I won't see her find it! Ah, but she will! My wife is a clever woman."

"It is all too sure that women confound us. That is so. But tell me, where did you hide the money?"

"So, you think I would tell you? But then, what would it matter? My wife already has found the money! To think, before the job in the refinery, I worked hard lifting beams, even using one of those shovels that smooth cement on a wall, carrying cement blocks; whatever the construction company wanted, I did. And now, after all this time, my wife finds the money and buys food and beer for the fiesta and all my relatives come – there must be fifty of them – and they eat up all that money in an hour.”

“Segundo, you should have spent the money right away, then it would not make you unhappy now.”

“Friend, do you try to make me feel better or worse?”

“I always tell the truth.”

“Eduardo, in truth, it is bad when a man does not have a job.”

“To have to work, that is worse.”

“But to be lazy like you, that disgusts me!”

“I enjoy life!”

“Like a lazy dog.”

Eduardo and Segundo stay in the shade of the lean-to, legs outstretched. Reina pokes one small finger in the sand.

“Look here, Reina de las Rosas, I will build a castle for you.” Eduardo shapes fine white sand into a cone, then lets particles sift through his fingertips. “See, it rains! What a fine day, but perhaps little queen, you have never seen the rain?”

“I have thirst for water from your canteen, Eduardo.”

“But first, water for the most precious of roses, La Reina.” Eduardo pours water into a cup and holds it to her lips. Water flows in rivulets over her chin as she swallows, resounding in her small body like plucked strings of the Venezuelan guitar, the *cuatro*.

“She is a good girl, Segundo.” Eduardo kisses Reina on the forehead. “I think if ever I should marry, it would be you, sweet rose.”

“My grandfather, you would!”

“She will be a beauty, Segundo. One can see that now. You must take care with her.”

"Already she costs me some thought. And all the relatives will swallow my hard-earned cash tonight. But then, what can one do? It is for the birthday of Reina de las Rosas, the sweet flower of my home. Though I have taken account, Eduardo, and one never gets back the money one puts into celebrations. Even the gifts do not pay for the food one's relatives eat."

"Do I see a bag of money replacing your head?"

Segundo frowned. "That is where I had the money hidden, in a little bag."

"Where did you say?"

"You don't think I would tell you?"

"Only what you don't tell your wife!"

Eduardo picks through the sand for bits of coral and shell. He holds before Reina a piece of staghorn coral marked with the laced intricacies of polyps and shaped like an animal, with forelegs and back, that comes alive as he sets a small clam shell over the neck, touching the edge so the head wags back and forth.

The men laugh as she watches with fascination.

"Come, Reina, let us look for things that are living." Segundo carries her in his arms as they rise and walk on through the sand. Waves break fresh and white edged against deepening blue water.

"Reina, see over there?"

A pelican soars, floating on currents of air. Suddenly, folding wings, the great bird dives straight into the bay, reappearing, flipping its large bill upward and with one gulp has a fish in its pouch. The pelican, accordion wings spread wide, beats against the water, gaining momentum in great flapping motions until it rises airborne, then flies in graceful sallies across the bay and back again.

"The pelican never errs. Always gets what it dives for."

"Such an ugly bird. And yet, what grace and power it possesses!"

"There is Salvatore's boat," says Segundo, pointing to the bay.

"The fishermen must be laying nets."

A few boards in the sand with a tarpaulin thrown over serve as a fishermen's hut. The sand slopes to the water and sticks rise in the shallows, forming a bait pen.

"There is El Sapo."

He limps toward them, his foot twisted.

"Sapo, what goes?"

"Has your luck been good?"

El Sapo holds out his hands, palms up, then shuffles toward the cliffs. High above, men on their haunches scan the sea, waiting, watching for the fish to come.

Eduardo and Segundo sit in the sand, Reina straddling Segundo's knee.

"He has the torso of a bull."

"He can outgrip any of the fishermen, I am told."

"No one makes jest of El Sapo."

"But for the foot, he could bring in the net by himself."

Soon fish are sighted. The sentinels give a signal. Two dories bob near shore. One maintains position, as the other boat moves quickly into the bay. Three men lower a net into the water in a great arc until a hundred meters are hung by cork floats in the bay.

A half dozen men who had been lounging on the deck of the old, sturdy *Pajaro* now wade to shore through water waist deep, hat brims rolled upward, pulled low on their foreheads. Five men hold one rope end while far down the shore, men scramble from the rocks to hold the other end of the rope. They pull the huge net to shore with all the strength of their being, wrestling in contest with the sea. The men, legs braced as a wedge, force the sea to yield. As the net is slowly wrung back from the water, sea spray mixes with the rich oil of sweat on sun-deepened skins. One by one, the men turn, the rope crossing their backs and shoulders, straining until they reach the coil of net growing ever higher on the beach. Then they return to the waves to pull again.

Finally, quiverings rise from the depths of the water. The men pull faster, with expectancy. When the net reaches the shallows, hundreds of white flickerings shoot the surface and the fishermen, silent until then, shout, "It is good!"

"Three hundred kilo."

"Three-fifty."

"Come, pull once more!"

Caught within the net are hundreds of squirming sardines and larger fish. Shouts of the fishermen toss back and forth in the sunlight of space and undulating sea, absorbed by the great movement of bodies, swooping gulls, rolling dories, and pelicans gathering at the net.

With one last effort the net is brought onto the sand. Sardines leap and twist vainly to regain the freedom lost within the net. Eduardo and Segundo press near. The sardines, five to six inches in length, brilliantly shining when pulled from the water, dull quickly in the air, tarnished by the jealous aura of the sun. Gulls fly greedily to the net, then rise into the air with small fish and shrimp and soft-shell crab. The fishermen carry buckets of sardines to the bait pen and collect larger fish for market. The too-small *coro-coro* and red snapper are thrown back to the sea. Pelicans rock in the shallows and fish swim to them.

El Sapo examines the net. The heavy mesh which snared sardines also caught seaweed and other creatures. "Nature couldn't decide what to do with this," he says, "feet, wings, and gills. And on its back, poisonous spines."

"A dogfish."

"Yes. And this, little one, is not as pretty as it looks." El Sapo holds a flat round fish for Reina to see. It is the size of a large coin, yellow with a black spot in the center. A small finger thrusts toward the fish.

"No, no, do not touch it! This one could give you a poisonous sting."

The fishermen yell, "Get him out, get him out!"

A pelican, flapping its wings, agitates other pelicans and drives them away while it lunges forward, catching fish after fish in its large beak.

"That one will leave none for us!"

"Get him, Sapo!"

"Yes, strike him, strike him!"

El Sapo strides through the sand toward the bird, holding a big stick. The pelican, spreading its wings, flops in the sand, shifting position just as El Sapo strikes. The other pelicans, alarmed, escape into the water, floundering momentarily, then gaining sufficient momentum, soar into the sky.

The hefty bird flops in circles in the sand, "*Vaya*, go, greedy one!"

"That bird is *borracho!* Drunk on fish."

"Hit it, hit it!" El Sapo strikes another blow. The pelican extends its great wings, beating feebly, but cannot rise.

"You have him, you have him!"

The bird is dazed. El Sapo grabs a wingtip and others help. The wingspan is wider than a man is tall. The head droops, blank eyes stare. The fishermen free the pelican and it staggers drunkenly. They laugh at the great bird, once so powerful, now feebly turning half circles in the sand.

"It is the greedy ones, like that pelican, that don't leave anything for the others, that get into trouble."

Eduardo and Segundo turn and walk back through the sand the way they came. "Segundo, have you forgotten to bathe the little queen?"

"So I have! And wouldn't my wife be mad, today being the birthday celebration of Reina de las Rosas." He tosses off his sandals and rolls up his pant legs. "Here, Reina, you shall have a bath."

He slips off her dress. Reina squeals as her father raises her high into the sky. "So, you don't like the sea? *Uno, dos, tres.* One, two, three!"

Reina shrieks each time she is plunged into the water. "Reina, up! Up! The sea won't get you. Not when your papa's here!"

He dries her with the little dress. "Let's go! Yes, and I return home a poor man, for surely my wife has found the money!"

"Look at it this way, Segundo—if you drink enough beer at the fiesta then you will not feel bad. As the father of Reina de las Rosas, you are a fortunate man."

"You are right, Eduardo. And tonight Reina shall have a fine first birthday celebration."

THE BIRTHDAY PARTY

Breeze-blown shadows and lights from Chinese lanterns play across tables in the patio of the de las Rosas family as voices within the *casa* flow into the velvet thickness of a tropic evening.

"Elena, did you count who is coming?"

"I counted the rented plates. Weren't there supposed to be fifty, Mama?"

"About that many are coming."

"Is Federico coming?"

"Of course he is coming! He is Reina's godfather."

"But I have never understood. Why is Federico Reina's godfather?"

"He is my nephew—you know that, Elena. He is very talented. That boy's voice is golden."

"Mama, he is not a boy! But is he going to sing for us tonight?"

"He said so. Well, we ought to have enough beer. I got your father to set the other cases behind the kitchen wall. José, did you get the ice?"

José, Gladis' lanky teenage son, nods at the kitchen doorway, swiping black hair from his forehead.

"Who left the pants hanging over a chair in the living room? Please get them out of there, José."

"Mama, is it time to put the empanadas in the oven?"

"No, Elena. But you aren't dressed yet! Hurry up now!"

"Oh, Mama, here comes Clarina!"

"I knew my sister would be early. She will insist that I leave the kitchen to her. But everything is almost ready."

"José," Gladis called from the kitchen door, "please hang the piñata."

"Is it filled, Mama?"

"The candy is under my bed. Hurry, now, but don't wake Reina. She is sleeping there."

"Clarina, here you are! So, your gallbladder is not bothering?"

"No more than usual, sister," said Clarina, out of breath. "The blood pressure is troubling, though, when I walk over here."

"José would have picked you up. He is going with Olivo's car for Eduardo and a girlfriend."

Clarina held a package wrapped in crinkled tissue. "Here is a gift for little Reina. Worked on it for two months! My hands aren't so quick anymore."

"Thank you! A crocheted dress for Reina. What a surprise! Come, Clarina, Segundo is on the patio. Come talk with him."

"But I am needed in the kitchen."

"Let her go, Mama, you can't do anything about her."

"Elena, what are you doing out here half dressed?"

"I can't get the dress zipped, Mama. I haven't worn it since Easter and it's too tight!" wailed Elena.

"That's enough, Elena! You'll have to hold in your breath. I'll get it on you."

"I hope so!"

"Go, Elena, quickly! Here comes Roberto with Linda and Olivo." Gladis hurried to the door.

"Good evening," Gladis said, as she hugged her sister and nodded to her brother-in-law.

"My car is here for José," said Olivo, "to pick up Eduardo and the girlfriend."

"Gladis, I thought I would get here early to help," said Linda.

"Our sister Clarina is already in the kitchen. She won't let anyone else in there."

"How is she?"

"As good as possible, considering that she always complains!"

"Roberto," said Linda, "give your aunt the little box."

The boy searches playfully through the pockets of his new pants. "Can't find it!" Roberto is Gladis' nephew, born three days after Elena. "Oh yes, here it is!"

"Can we open it now? Come, Segundo is sitting out back. Segundo, see what Linda and Olivo have brought for Reina's birthday! The sacred medal of Guadalupe."

"As precious as little Reina de las Rosas. And where is she?" asked Olivo.

"Sleeping," replied Gladis.

"Mama!" Elena called from the interior of the house. "Mama, come here!"

Gladis left the others in the yard and found Elena in the small second bedroom, struggling, hands behind her back, pulling at the zipper of her dress. "Oh, Mama," said Elena, turning to her mother in desperation, "I can't get it on! What shall I do?"

"Now Elena, don't get upset!" Gladis worked at the dress from the back, her hands strong, holding the dress at the waist, trying to pull the material together. "You're getting fat, Elena."

"I am not! I'm still growing."

"Then, why don't you wear the dress your cousin left here? She isn't coming from the city for a month, anyhow."

"Oh, Mama, do you think I could?" She zipped up the dress of yellow rayon. It fit just snugly enough.

"You'll have to wear a belt or sash with it. It looks much too old, Elena."

"Oh, Mama, it does not!" said Elena, pleased with the sight of herself in a small mirror.

In the yard, Olivo expounded on the thought that all troubles come from money."

"No," said Segundo, "better said, all troubles come from the lack of it."

"Would you like a cold beer, Olivo?" asked Gladis.

"Where do the good things in life come from without money?" queried Segundo, eyeing Gladis, knowing she had found the bag he had hidden under the bed.

Olivo took the beer. Gladis brought one to Segundo. "A little beer in the stomach settles the mind," he said.

"Segundo," asked Gladis, "is José going to pick up Rosita?"

"I told Eduardo that José would drive him and a girlfriend. But he can get Rosita, too."

"And Rosita, like a tigress, will be dragging Federico here tonight by the nape of the neck," said Segundo.

"That is not so! He is Reina's godfather," said Gladis.

"He is my wife's nephew," said Segundo, "and Reina's godfather only because we ran out of other relatives for the baptism."

"That is not so, Segundo!" Gladis frowned. "That boy is talented. He could be a good provider for Reina someday."

"My wife has a fondness for Federico, her ill-tempered sister's child," he commented to Olivo.

"If he would marry Esperanza…" said Gladis. "She is coming tonight. Hadn't I told you?"

"Is her family coming too? Are you sure?" asked Segundo.

"Yes. Esperanza will come if she thinks Federico will be here. As a favor to my sister, Rosita, I arranged it. Besides, Esperanza and Elena are good friends, since Elena works at the father's store. Good pay for a girl just fifteen. Esperanza comes into the shop and talks to Elena, assuming that Elena will pass on to Federico anything she might say about him. My Elena is a sensible girl, though, and doesn't try to encourage her. If Esperanza gets it into her head that Federico likes her, she is sure to drive him away!"

"I think she needs a lot of discouragement."

"But," said Gladis, "the only sensible thing for Federico is to marry that girl."

"But love is not sensible."

"Neither is Federico," said Gladis. "He has a chance to get into a family business that any other young man would be anxious to have. He has a good life practically handed to him, but no, Federico refuses to take the burden of himself off Rosita's shoulders."

"He understands one thing: that Esperanza is no great wit."

"Is marriage something to be clever at, make jokes about?"

"Humor helps," said Segundo. "Marriage is a laughable business."

"Segundo," said Gladis, "heaven knows you are a joker! Esperanza is all right. Not bad looking."

"A doll's face," said Segundo.

"Shuu. There's a car. Isn't that her family right now?"

"They all have arrived in one car."

Segundo met them at the open door. Light from the interior guided the guests through a path of oil barrels filled with purchased earth that turned the front of the house into a garden of croton, periwinkle, hibiscus, and the scent of gardenia.

"Señor, Señora, how are you?"

"Good evening!"

Esperanza scowled. She had just come from the beauty salon, her brown hair curling precisely over rouged cheeks, gold bracelets clinking at her wrists. "Someone's been sitting on my dress," she said, "I'm wrinkled!"

"No you aren't," said Gladis, noticing the smooth fair skin of her face.

"We all got in that car, somehow!" said Esperanza, straightening her tightly fitting new red dress. She was annoyed with her three young brothers who were pushing past her at the door. "I saw Rosita on the way, waiting for a car. Is Federico coming?"

"Federico is Reina's godfather," said Gladis. "Did you know that?"

"No," said Esperanza, her brown eyes brightening almost to the shine of her gloss-blue eye shadow.

"Boys, go out to the patio where the piñata is," said Gladis to Esperanza's young brothers.

Her parents sat down formally in the small living room. The pink walls seemed to pull the room stiflingly close around them. Gladis tried to lighten the conversation. Esperanza sat on the arm of the sofa, facing the front door while Elena chattered to her about the yellow dress she wore—the length, the fit, how she disliked the sash her mother insisted that she wear.

"It's okay," said Esperanza, who was listening to Gladis say, "Sr. Hernandez has given Federico some of his songs for first performance. Federico is doing well, no? Singing at the hotel."

"I've heard," said Olivo, "that his only thoughts are for the women."

Gladis shot him a sharp stare. "You are right, he doesn't have his mother's head for business. She has done well with her sewing."

"Mama!"

"What, Elena?"

"I can see from here, Esperanza's brothers climbed the tree and let the piñata drop and the candy fell out and they are eating it!"

"Well then, they won't eat so much of everything else! Elena, did you put the empanadas in the oven?"

"Yes, but I forgot them!"

"They are not forgotten," came Clarina's voice from the kitchen.

"Thanks to God, Clarina!"

"No, thanks to me!" said Clarina.

"Ah, smell the empanadas!" said Gladis. She had prepared the golden pastries herself and filled them with shredded beef, boiled eggs, raisins, and her piquant sauce. "Elena, pass them to the guests, please."

"Look! Here come Rosita and Federico."

"*Buenas noches!* Good evening! A good night for the birthday party," said Federico. "The moon is almost full."

"But where is your cuatro, Federico?"

"I have it here," he said, pulling the four-stringed instrument from behind his back, moving to the patio.

"Rosita, how are you, my sister?" asked Gladis.

"I'm here. Is everyone else?"

"Yes, if you mean Esperanza and her family. They're on the patio."

"That son of mine," said Rosita, shaking her head.

"Now Rosita, you know that you are proud of Federico."

Segundo brought a glass of scotch and ice to Federico. "You always sing better with a little scotch."

"Salud to Reina!" said Federico, raising the glass. "Reina de las Rosas, who makes one year today. To her, many years of happiness. Salud to the little queen. May she grow into a beautiful rose."

"That was well said, Federico."

"But where is she, the little one?" asked Federico.

"Asleep," said Gladis, "in our bedroom."

"I'll tip-toe in to see how much she has grown since last week."

Later, Esperanza sidled up to Federico. "Are you going to sing for us?" she asked, her skin blushing even deeper than the new blush she had so carefully applied. "You have such a beautiful voice, Federico."

"Esperanza!" sighed Federico with an exasperation that Esperanza could not grasp.

"You should be on television."

"I'd live in Caracas."

"Marry rich, then, Federico," said Olivo, with a hint of mockery.

Esperanza lowered her head, "You have a golden voice."

"That's what I have been saying, Olivo," said Segundo, "all our problems come from money."

"The lack of it, you said. There are troubles of the heart, Segundo, that money cannot cure."

"But a good wife and family make one rich, Federico."

"You have said so many times. I thought it was the women who cause heart trouble."

"Troubles of the heart, you mean," said Segundo.

Federico sauntered toward the bar.

"If Federico had money he would go off to the big city and become famous as a singer," said Olivo.

"But he can still go," said Segundo. "Federico is no fool."

Gladis came in from the kitchen. "Has José gone for Eduardo? Did you say he was bringing a girlfriend, Segundo?"

"That is what he said today at the beach. He describes her in glowing terms as his new flame."

"Counting the two of them and Olivo's seven, and nine with us, plus my cousins, a few friends, that is about thirty-five, and Esperanza. Her family makes six, now, that is forty-one, and the musicians, the *conjunto*, five more… and the neighbors."

"Here comes Eduardo now," said Segundo.

Eduardo gave Gladis a kiss and Segundo *un abrazo*, a back-patting embrace, then turned to the girl who had followed him in. Her hair was a dark wreath around an attractive face. Eduardo turned to her, smiling broadly. "I'd like to present Lela."

"Much pleasure," they said, shaking hands.

To Lela, Gladis said, "Have you been here long?"

"No, not long."

And do you like it here?"

"Oh, I like it," she said, "yes!"

"You are working?"

"I work as a hostess at the Lone Palm Restaurant. That is where I met Eduardo."

"I haven't been there yet," said Gladis, "but I hope to go. Tonight we will eat roasted chicken and barbequed goat ribs. And birthday cake."

"Perfect!" said Lela.

"Gladis, you are a wonder," said Eduardo and kissed her again on the cheek.

"Enough of that, Eduardo!" said Segundo. "Let's get some beer, or would you rather have scotch?"

"Beer. Where is everyone?"

"On the patio."

"And where is the little princess," asked Eduardo, "the joy of my heart, Reina de las Rosas, whose birthday we have come to celebrate?"

"She is sleeping in the bedroom."

"The day at the beach tired her. But for her we celebrate, the little flower of my soul."

"Eduardo, you are positively poetic!" exclaimed Segundo.

As Gladis returned to the kitchen, Eduardo said, "Well, Segundo, apparently your wife found and spent the bag of money!"

"Yes, friend, that is how it is."

"Shall I put my little gift here with the others on the table?"

"Yes, thank you, Eduardo."

"She brings much joy, Segundo. A beautiful rose."

Segundo led Eduardo and Lela to the back of the house. Guests were seated informally about the patio and at long tables set for the late evening meal. They walked into a soft breeze, the bobbing lights, and the strumming of the cuatro.

Lela froze. She saw Federico and heard him singing the old favorite, "Noche de Ronda":

"Dile que le quiero… Tell her that I love her."

Federico possessed the song, fondling the words. Lela was unable to move forward on her own, but Eduardo pulled her over to a table where she was introduced. The women smiled thinly, the men eyed her, assessing what kind of woman she was. But Lela paid no attention. She was absorbed in Federico's presence. He was saying, "I want to dedicate this song to the two beautiful daughters of my Aunt Gladis and her good husband, Segundo – to Elena, and especially, Reina de las Rosas, who makes one year this evening – 'Maria Elena.'"

There were sighs of approval. Federico began:

"I want to sing for you, Reina,

my most beautiful song – today

you are queen – of my heart."

Lela stared at Federico. He had not seen her, was not aware of her.

"Mujer de mi ilusión… Woman of my illusion."

Esperanza, listening at the nearest table, turned toward Federico in a dramatic pose, bosom up, chin up.

Elena disappeared behind a flamboyant tree in the small yard. Roberto, her cousin and childhood friend, came to her and climbed up on the cement block wall that surrounded the house. Roberto coaxed Elena to climb up with him but her tight skirt kept her from hiking her knee up as she might have when she was younger, to pull herself onto the wall to sit by him.

Instead, she stood below Roberto, twining her fingers, preening. Roberto liked what he saw, her face turned up to him, the curve of her breasts in the yellow dress. He jumped down and pressed her to the tree, kissing her until she struggled free, giggling, and ran over to the tables to sit down in front of Federico. She turned back smiling and saw Roberto leaning against the wall, watching her.

Gladis came to her and said, "Elena, I want you to set the tables now. And be careful with that dress. It belongs to your cousin. You can't afford to snag it, or worse, tear it!"

"But you said I could wear it, Mama!"

"Yes, I know! Elena, please check the kitchen. Be sure the food is ready to serve. Clarina won't let me in there. That's how she is!"

"Yes, Mama!"

Gladis glanced across the tables to Federico. He was intent in his song, but acknowledged her with a nod, then closed his eyes on the tender

"to die for love is to be born…"

For all the disagreements, his fights over Esperanza, Federico cared for his aunt Gladis and her family, perhaps more than his own mother, who seemed to be shut away, struggling in some medieval Spanish darkness. Federico set the cuatro down. His throat was dry. He went to the bar for another scotch on ice and found Esperanza at his elbow.

"How beautiful your song, Federico!"

"Eh, you think so?"

"Oh, yes, of course!" She waited for Federico to say something, but he turned from her and struck up a conversation with Olivo.

Esperanza was not offended. She already was reliving the

encounter, playing it again in her mind as she sat down by her parents.

Gladis held a plate of empanadas. Esperanza's mother took several at once, obviously hungry. Gladis thought anxiously that she ought to get the food to the tables.

The Chinese lanterns trembled as chocolate clouds drifted across the moon. Edges of the tablecloths blew onto the tables if not pinned down by plates or silverware. Paper cups rolled willy-nilly. No one minded. Guests were happy with the mix of alcohol and easy talk to fill the long evening hours.

Roberto sat on the wall joking with other youths, waiting, eyeing the back door for Elena to come out.

Federico, filing between tables, caught his Aunt Gladis from the back by reaching around her arms and took empanadas from the plate she held. "Oh, my little aunt, what a beneficent angel you are. I'm hungry!"

"We'll eat soon, nephew. How is it with you and Esperanza?"

"It isn't. Impossible question. Impossible – I hesitate to say – woman. That would be overstating her."

"Federico," said his aunt, "at close range, I am beginning to agree with you."

Eduardo approached through a narrow space between tables and chairs. Lela followed him, unseen by Federico until that moment. Federico stepped back, completely surprised.

But Lela had seen Federico. She was prepared. She would not betray him. He slowly comprehended her in this setting so familiar to him, in which she was an intruder. Lela returned his stare and let a smile slip tentatively from the corner of her lips, but Federico refused the acknowledgement. If Federico was going to ignore her, she could ignore him as well. But as they passed between tables, her breasts slightly brushed his arm, exciting her.

She looked at Eduardo. He had caught none of it. She liked Eduardo, but their relationship was different. He knew her as the new waitress at the Lone Palm, a girl from the mountains. But she was learning fast—learning how to live in town.

Plates of food were passed around the tables as Eduardo found chairs for Lela and himself. Federico was persuaded to take up the cuatro again. Familiar words of songs enveloped the evening. Talk quieted while the guests ate at the birthday celebration of Reina de las Rosas, who was asleep in the bedroom.

Federico glared at Lela. She was desirable sitting there, talking to Eduardo. What line did Eduardo have on her? He would find out. He would eliminate that *macho* from Lela's life. When he finished the next song he would have a beer on top of the scotch. He knew that was dangerous, would set him off wrong, but he didn't care.

Esperanza came with a plate of food to sit near Federico as he sang. Young Elena sat with her until Roberto came over and pulled her away, led her back under the flamboyant tree.

Gladis had seen them. It was her duty to keep Elena constantly in her eye from now on. Let her be flattered by male attention, but watch her always. This time of blossoming in a girl's life was so short, the freedom so brief, then came a woman's giving in to a lifetime of duties. Gladis, herself, was lucky. Segundo was easy. She could get what she wanted, usually; even if money was scarce, she managed. And now Elena and José helped with jobs. She kept a good home she was proud of and three beautiful children. That was a blessing.

Little Reina, the baby who had surprised her later in life, was a greater joy than she could have imagined. Even the delivery, just a year ago, had been surprisingly easy after two big babies close together when she was a girl, just turned eighteen when José came and Elena a year later.

The plate was almost empty of empanadas. Clarina had relinquished the kitchen, her plate high with food. Now it would be easier for Gladis to pass around the last of the food which, she thought ruefully, had taken her five days of shopping and preparation. Then there would be the ravages of the party to be cleaned, discovering cigarette butts, scraps of food under furniture and bottles in the yard. But the party was going well.

Gladis passed food once more. She saw Roberto by the wall and Elena sitting on top of it, playfully swinging new shoes toward Roberto's chest. He grabbed a shoe, pulling it off, holding it behind his back. Elena screeched, laughing. The attachment of cousins was often close. From now on Gladis must try to pull the bonds apart. Elena at fifteen would be a *quinceanera* and have a party to announce her coming of age, her availability as a future marriage prospect.

Elena had been the infant that Reina now was. Soon Reina would be grown. Gladis went inside the house. The child was beginning to stir—crying, then howling to see if anyone was near. "Reina, you are awake, birthday child!"

Gladis washed Reina's face, moistening the dark curls on her forehead and then took from a hanger a dress of starched white cotton with a full-gathered skirt and short puffed sleeves, with a bodice trimmed in bands of lace.

On the patio, the conjunto was setting up with harp, maracas, cuatro, and guitar. Soon the dancing would begin.

Esperanza, all broad curves in the red dress, hurried after Federico. She followed him right to the door of the bathroom. Well, she would wait, though the music pulled her attention from the door.

When Federico came out, he said, "What are you doing here?"

"Waiting," said Esperanza. There was nothing for her to do but go into the bathroom, and that meant Federico had escaped her once again. She would never be able to wiggle out of her underpinnings, but she could smooth down new curls and apply more eye shadow.

Federico strode through the small house, ducking through doorways. He did this instinctively. His height must have come from his father – whoever he was – who had sent his mother's life tumbling in the missile that became his own life, even his own big bones. Bending under the door frame as he came from the hall, Federico searched for Lela. He couldn't see her anywhere and he was afraid that she might have left with that what's-his-name, Eduardo.

He knew that Eduardo was a friend of the family, especially

Segundo. Gladis, he saw, was fond of Eduardo, and Lela, he couldn't tell. She was his and not his in the same moment. That confused him. What held her back from him when he came to her room? Certainly she had sought him out on the street. She'd said so herself.

Federico didn't see her in the crowd. It made him mad to think that she would have left with that peanut, Eduardo. He had seen the silly way he grinned at Lela and he could have hit the guy in the mouth right then, but he had been in mid-verse of a song and almost forgot the words – words so well known to him that he didn't have to think consciously while singing – and yet that *enano*, that runt, nearly made him forget the song.

What kind of game was Lela playing with him anyway? Did she know he would be here tonight? Had he ever told her about his family, how he was *padrino*, godfather to Reina? No, she must have come with Eduardo by chance. Only in this way had he found out that she went out with someone else—when she'd promised!

Federico went to the bar. Just one more scotch and ice to settle his nerves and then he would join the conjunto. The musicians were ready to play another set. Couples surrounded the polished cement floor of the patio, waiting for the music to begin.

He saw Lela and Eduardo standing together. When she turned to him, he shot her the coldest stare possible. How could he hate her? But in that moment he thought he did. He could feel his hands closing around the neck of that *malandrino*, that rascal. He struck three harsh chords on the cuatro and the music began. It reverberated off the aluminum roof of the patio, rolling in waves into the night—pulsating with the hearts of the dancers, drowning them in the intoxication of the beat.

Federico was determined not to, but his eyes wandered to Lela, her oscillating bottom, the slender legs curving nicely in her only pair of heels. And the green blouse with the tiny buttons down the front. She had worn that with him, when she sat across the table at the Italian restaurant. Since she got the job at the Lone Palm, he hadn't seen her as much. She said she had to work nights.

The group played a cumbia. Federico sang:

"...the beautiful negress, how she dances,

she seems to rise up out of the sea..."

The tempo quickened, her movements too, in a tight black skirt. She danced well with Eduardo and that sickened Federico. There she was, swinging her hips to the cumbia with that *truhán*, that scoundrel.

In the next song he tried to send the meaning directly to Lela:

"...*Mi tierra*, how beautiful

all my feelings are in this song.

I want to express the enchantment

of that beautiful land."

When the song was over he set his cuatro carefully in a corner. He saw Eduardo head to the bar and went over to Lela. "What are you doing here with him?"

Lela looked up, shaking her head 'no.'

"No what, Lela? Speak up!"

"It's not what you think."

"How do I know? I watched you dancing with him." He grabbed her wrist and led her into the shadows at the back of the house.

"Can't I dance with whom I want?"

"Not when I pay for your room. Lela, listen to me! You keep away from him and the others. Do you understand me?"

She nodded. He forced her to him, holding her wrist, his other hand pushing into the small of her back. She tried to lean away.

"Why won't you kiss me now?!" She rolled her face from side to side.

"Because you're mad at me! That's why!"

"Lela, you promised!"

"Don't you think I can keep a promise, if I want? How should I feel when you don't trust me? I see what you think of me!" Lela broke free, tripping on empty beer bottles, struggling to her feet. "You will have to treat me better than this!"

"Lela!" Federico called after her, frustration breaking into tears in his eyes. Why couldn't he rid himself of the slut? Find somebody else. Forgodsake, not that stupid Esperanza! But some woman of Spanish blood, light-skinned, not so mixed as Lela. But what was he anyway? Half and half, his mother said. A father he had never seen, a sailor named Fred, who came in a ship in the early days of the big war when the oil fields were opening. The frontier days. Now people were being corralled, fenced in. He hoped for some escape for himself, Caracas and a nightclub. He leaned against the wall and told himself he would have gone already if it hadn't been for Lela.

Federico caught the two of them together, just as the conjunto was tuning up again.

Lela's eyes widened as he strode toward them. She tried to calm him with her gaze, to hold him to it, but she knew that Federico had gone over an emotional cliff, plummeting him she knew not where. He was impetuous and that uncertainty in Federico had frightened and also fascinated her. And what was he doing now? He was saying to Eduardo, "Leave her alone! You understand?"

"You can't say that to me, you have no justification!"

But the level of alcohol coursing through Federico's veins made him extravagant, everything dramatized. He was pulling them toward rapids where neither Lela nor Eduardo wished to go.

"You have no justification!" repeated Eduardo.

"Just this," said Federico, twisting Eduardo's left arm behind his back. Eduardo strained under the pain. Federico was strong and also drunk. "Lela belongs to me!"

"Your property?" said Eduardo, fighting back the only way he could, with his mind, against this fellow—and he knew in that moment he would have to have it out with Lela, too, or just drop her. But that was exactly what Federico would want him to do.

Swiftly Eduardo's right hand shot out for Federico's jaw, grazing him. Enraged, Federico let go of Eduardo's wrist and swung at him with his fist.

They saw that the guests had gathered just outside the periphery of action and knew they were on stage and let go with the best they had. No one tried to interfere or break up the fight, knowing instinctively that pent-up energy must be expended and when it was, the fight would end. Eduardo punched right and left. Federico with one blow to Eduardo's jaw sent him sprawling over a table, crashing in a clatter of dishes and silverware.

Eduardo pushed away plates with his arms, trying to get up from the remains of the dinner. Federico fell on him, following the face with fist blows, but as he did so, the weight of the two men upset the table and they tumbled to the ground—silverware, cups, and plates tossed about, the tablecloth draped on their heads.

No one had time to recover when Gladis appeared in the midst of the guests with Reina in her arms, the child dressed beautifully in white and ribbons.

"What has happened here?" asked Gladis, so calmly curious that, at the sight of the child so sweetly innocent and the dumped table so incongruous, the crowd burst into laughter. But the laughter, sudden to her ears, frightened Reina and she shrieked in fear. That made the crowd laugh more. Tension passed, the party would go on.

Federico and Eduardo stared glassily at each other, their dislike more intense for the ridiculous position into which they had fallen, both vowing to stay clear of Lela.

Elena, who with Roberto's help had jumped from the wall when the fight began, realized just then that she had torn the skirt of her cousin's dress. "Ah, *dios!* What could be worse!"

Eduardo's lip was swelling. He wondered where Lela was, but Segundo told him that she wanted to leave, so José was driving her back to her room. Eduardo apologized to Segundo. "Believe me, friend, I didn't know that she was involved with Federico. Otherwise,

I swear, I never would have brought her here to the party."

"I believe you, Eduardo."

"I just met her a few nights ago at the Lone Palm."

"Yes, she works there, doesn't she?" said Segundo. "Haven't I warned you, friend, that it is easier to get burned by a new flame than an old fire?"

"Then you accept my apology before I leave?"

"Of course."

The musicians reached for their instruments. Federico brushed away what crumbs he could, picked up his cuatro, and joined the rest in "Cumpleaños Feliz."

The guests sang "Happy Birthday, dear Reina," and someone wiped a small tear from her cheek. Reina de las Rosas, whose birthday by the hour now gone into yesterday, was the center of attention. She was passed around the crowd, cuddled, kissed, and coaxed by all to mimic them, to repeat simple words, to look for approval in the eyes of her audience, to look to those who would give her love.

Then the dancing began in earnest, the guests forgetting all but the enjoyment of keeping to the delicious Latin beat of the music.

Los Tres Golpes

"*Hola*, Eduardo!"

"*Hola*, Oscar!"

"Well, what do you think of Ricardo's place?"

"A good place for a restaurant, here on the corner. People will look in and decide they want to come in to eat. But why does Ricardo call it 'Los Tres Golpes'?"

"Like baseball, three strikes—you're out!"

"But that is an unlucky name."

"Name or not, Eduardo, what brings you here this evening? Come, sit at this table."

"I got an invitation to the opening of this restaurant. And did you get one too, Oscar?"

"Yes, and I am not one to pass up a free meal."

"Nor I. But I don't know why I was invited. I don't know Ricardo very well. He hasn't lived here long, has he, Oscar?"

"No, but long enough to know that you are a respectable man in this town, Eduardo. Ricardo is not much of a fool. He wants to make

Los Tres Golpes a big thing. He knows that you will bring important people to his new restaurant."

"So, Oscar, why are you invited?"

"I gave Ricardo a little help starting this place."

"What? Don't tell me you've started raising chickens!"

"No, but did you notice this table you are sitting at? Very nice, yes? Covered with a red and white checked tablecloth. Well, Eduardo, you know that yard on the far side of the oil refinery? Near the warehouse? Where old equipment is dumped? Well, the night watchman, Guido, is a good friend of mine. I give him a little money and Ricardo gives me more—not promises, but cash for these six tables."

"You old buzzard!"

"They would be ruined in the rain, anyway."

"What do you mean, rain? It never rains here!"

"True, but look over there. Lightning to the west. Feel how still the air is? Not blowing from the east as usual. If the wind reverses, it might bring rain tonight. Eight months and three days since last it rained."

"That long?"

"Exactly, Eduardo. That is an important matter with me! I have a bet with my brother-in-law. He says that it won't rain for eleven months. Says he had a dream about it. He can dream all he wants, but the sky over there is dark, so I might win thirty bolivars cash tonight, though my brother-in-law never pays up. Never has money. I always try to keep a little pocket change on me."

"I think you pocketed some from the oil company, Oscar!"

"They will never miss it. The company is rich. Guido, the watchman, says they don't count the old tables, anyway."

"I wonder where Ricardo got money for this place?"

"Shuuuu. Here he comes!"

"Welcome, señores!"

"Buenas noches, Ricardo! It is a pleasure to come to your new restaurant this evening. We will toast your great success! But where is the wine?"

"You come a little early, señores. Many people are coming here this evening. But tell me, what do you think of my restaurant? Fancy enough, eh, Eduardo? And Oscar, do not the tablecloths do justice to the tables?"

"Yes, Ricardo, but I am interested in what you put on the tablecloth besides the dripped candles in empty wine bottles. What's for dinner?"

"The meal will complement the tables, I assure you, Oscar. A very special feast tonight, my good patron. Fresh bird, especially tender, cooked with delicate and expert care, surrounded by steaming mounds of rice."

"Arroz con Pollo, but that is a common dish."

"Uncommon in my hands! Think of the bird, roasted to perfection, a golden hue with juices bubbling just under the surface, and rice, each tender morsel flavored with an exquisite combination of garlic and saffron. Each bite more tantalizing than the last. To think on it makes one's appetite greater."

"Ricardo, don't keep us expecting the dinner too long!"

"Then, señores, if you will permit me, I must get back to the kitchen. I am afraid there will be a slight delay. That young burro, Manuel, has not come yet to install the grill, so I must cook only with the oven. But a fine oven it is, I assure you!"

"Are you sure that Manuel has finished that electrician's course? If not, then our dinner will be late!"

"Now that Ricardo is gone, Oscar, I ask you again, where does he get money to open this restaurant?"

"Some place it will be if it rains! Feel that wind from the west?"

"It blows with force."

"Remember the clever fellow who had his shop on this open corner, right in this very place? He had a good business until exactly eight months and three days ago when last it rained."

"Is that so?"

"Yes. Washed him out! I mean to say, the wind blew rain on all the bolts of dress material and ruined everything."

"Poor fellow. What happened to him?"

"Ran away. They say he bought everything on credit. But here come Guido and my brother-in-law."

"Buenas noches!"

"Hola, Oscar, Eduardo!"

"Good evening, señores," says Oscar, "Don't be anxious, if you are hungry. It will be some time before we eat. Ricardo is still cooking in the kitchen. But when he comes in, ask him for some wine, Guido, and we will toast his good fortune on the opening of his restaurant, Los Tres Golpes. After all, we deserve the wine for helping him—by coming here this evening."

"I believe you are right, Oscar, there is lightning to the west."

"Yes, Eduardo, what did I tell you? And then, brother-in-law, when it rains, you will owe me cash."

"Owe you is right! I don't have any change on me."

"Didn't I tell you, Eduardo? My brother-in-law never pays up."

"So, I am short of cash, Oscar, but let me tell you the surest bet to win yet! I have never seen anything like it, the way that cock of Doctor Martinez fights. That is the best fighting cock that I have seen, absolutely, without doubt."

"You have seen it fight, brother-in-law?"

"Last Saturday in the arena. It went for the eyes. A real fighter. Doctor Martinez gives special handling to that one cock, though he has several. He lets it fight only once a month. Now, that is a good tip, brother-in-law. Worth about thirty bolivars, I think."

"What did you say is the name of his best fighting cock?"

"I will tell you when it rains."

"Doesn't Doctor Martinez live near here?"

"Yes, and he is as rich as the foreigners. You can't tell from the street, but his house covers almost half of the next block and there he quarters his fighting cocks in the courtyard."

"I think I hear them from here."

"Here comes Manuel. Hola! How are you, Manuel?"

"Fine, thank you, Eduardo and señores, but I am looking for Ricardo. I promised to install the electric grill, and here it is almost time for dinner. And I was an invited guest, too! Have you seen him?"

"I think he is in the kitchen."

"Sounds like he has some fresh chickens out there."

"Brother-in-law, I see drops of rain. Now what is the name of that cock?"

"Well, let me think!"

"Look! Lightning again."

"And here comes little Salas, the big policeman!"

"Good evening, Salas, and why do you come here?"

"Have you seen Ricardo?"

"He was with us a while ago."

"Isn't he in the kitchen?"

"Here comes Doctor Martinez, running!"

"He seems angry."

"He is so furious that I can't understand what he is saying."

"Something about his cocks."

"Five cocks, he says. Five cocks gone!"

"Worth two thousand? For the cocks?"

"Where is Ricardo?"

"We thought he was in the kitchen, Salas."

"Here comes the west wind. Brother-in-law, it is starting to rain! Help me move these tables. Come, Guido, help! The rain will soak everything! Eight months and three days. What did I tell you?"

"Did anyone see Ricardo in the kitchen?"

"Better open the oven!"

"For the birds or Ricardo? He is sitting on the fire, no?"

"And what is the name of that cock, that 'good tip,' brother-in law?"

"¡Ay! Here comes Manuel, flying out of the kitchen, chased by a bird!"

"A cock after him!"

"Watch out! You can't catch those fighters."

"Out of the way, here he comes!"

"Run, Manuel! Quick, let him pass!"

"See those feathers fly!"

"What a handsome bird!"

"Ferocious! Don't let one catch you by the tail!"

"Here comes Doctor Martinez—make way!"

"Excuse me, gentlemen—I've got to catch that bird!"

"Rice and fighting cock. That's a tough dish!"

"An expensive meal!"

"I bet Ricardo is sorry he got those 'chickens.'"

"Manuel, you couldn't catch a cock for the grill?"

"Doctor Martinez is rounding them up. Listen to that squawking!"

"But where is Ricardo?"

"Gone!"

"Psst! Oscar!"

"Yes Eduardo, what is it?"

"Listen, while you were moving the tables, I heard Salas mention something about tables missing."

"In that case, I am leaving, *amigo.* Buenas noches, Eduardo!"

"Buenas noches, Oscar!"

"Say, Eduardo…"

"What, Salas?"

"Come over here. You say you saw Ricardo in the kitchen when you came in?"

"Not in the kitchen. He was right here talking with us. That is the bad luck of it! No arroz con pollo for dinner. And you were an invited guest too, Salas?"

"Yes. I didn't know about the cocks until I walked in here. Now I've got to stand guard in case Ricardo tries to come back for something. Some job, too, in this rain!"

"You know, Salas," said Eduardo, "Los Tres Golpes, like beisbol— three strikes and you are out!"

Jorge Fernando Montez

The sun was on his shoulder. He glanced at his new gold watch. The time was exactly 8:14 in the morning. Flipping a ring of keys as he approached the office door, he noticed a taxi waiting at the curb.

His eyes fell on the lettering on the glass door:

Ministerios De Relaciones Interiores

Estado Falcon, Venezuela

Jorge smiled, pleased with himself. Yes, Jorge Fernando Montez was a clerical official of the government, a typist in the *Cedula* office. He typed identification papers for citizens and processed papers for foreigners: Italian, French, Arab, Japanese, English, German, Dutch, and the North Americans. It was just such an encounter with foreigners that Jorge enjoyed most and, as he opened the door, he saw that certainly, it was an American in the taxi.

They were amusing and impatient. He knew that despite their pleading, their anger, no matter how perturbed they became, their papers, their official *cedulas*, would not be ready for several months, or more accurately, half a year.

As Jorge walked through the waiting room, an acrid smell of stale bodies and yesterday's dust sprang to his nostrils. He opened overhead windows and switched on two light bulbs and a ceiling fan. The fan, on occasion, had startled Jorge, whirling like a flying machine over his desk, but he was grateful to have the fan because the waiting room of the *Ministerios De Relaciones Interiores* was the hottest building in town. He endured the small discomforts, the incessant chattering, the bawling infants—endured it all for the greater importance of his job, the prestige and, he admitted to himself, the control of others that it gave him, not to mention the high, though not nearly high enough, salary.

Jorge sat down, elbows on the table that served as his desk, and gazed at the rows of chairs facing him, standing like soldiers at attention, recruits that had not yet broken ranks, had not been shifted from line by impatient hands or kicked by swinging feet—chairs that waited in servitude to the citizens of the country and foreigners, the heavy bottoms, thin trousers, the flower-blossomed skirts, and the weight of visiting dignitaries.

The American was the first to come in. She carefully closed the door behind her. Jorge called out, "No, no, leave the door open."

She opened the door again, peering quizzically at Jorge. He smiled broadly, his best smile, and nodded to her as a father might a child who awaited his approval. He appraised the woman now under his command. She was good looking enough, not bad, but plain and pale, her breasts flat, not enough flesh at the hips. And she had that peculiarly blanched American look of boiled potatoes. Jorge was a rice and *picante* man. He stared at her until she sat down and averted her eyes by pulling some papers from her handbag.

Yes, he enjoyed dealing with Americans. Especially the women. He was determined not to start working on her papers until the other officials had come and were seated at their typewriters, but it became increasingly difficult to seem occupied.

The American eyed him, he felt, with a certain respect and the curiosity of a newcomer to his country, his countrymen, and of course, himself.

Jorge had been pleasantly surprised at his reflection in the mirror this morning. His forehead was broad, a mark of intelligence, his black hair combed back smoothly; a thin moustache and a gold watch added much to his appearance as a man of some position and finance.

He found an old handkerchief in the drawer and dusted his typewriter. The American sighed and observed the ceiling fan. She read several times through papers in her handbag. Was she deliberately trying to avoid him? He made a clucking noise with his tongue and that made her raise her head.

At 8:39 his partners arrived and the room filled with people. The American sat in a front chair. When all of the seats but three were full, exactly fifteen, Jorge rose, tapped the table, and made a speech. "Quiet everyone! In order to be finished by noon, please come quickly when your name is called. If you have not done so, leave your name and request slip with me."

Jorge acknowledged the American. She was squinting at him. Yes, she was relying on him. He walked over, took her papers, and carefully tucked them under others on his desk. Then he began the long, repetitious questions: name, age, residence?

When he noticed her again, the American was thrashing her arms about. Swatting flies? Others were content to sit, letting flies crawl, quiet except for constant chatter. A few were slumped on chairs, asleep. The American pointed to herself. He nodded yes, in a moment, perhaps.

He continued questioning the curvaceous Graciela who was leaving the country for a weekend. He wondered with whom and, for a moment, conjectured such a venture for himself. "And what is your present address?"

Graciela answered coyly, "You know, the Hotel."

He glanced at the American. She sat cross-legged, swinging one sandaled foot around in a circle and above her the fan rotated with a soft whumming sound. He gave *gracias a dios* for the fan, for without the breeze, however slight, it would be impossible for a gentleman like himself to work at all.

When she turned to him, he gave her a deliberate smile, raising one eyebrow, but she wasn't going to play the game. Sometimes the local girls simply got mad, but the Americans, one could not always tell how to handle them.

"Señora, Americana, *adelante!*" he called, adding smoothly with just the proper lilt of indifference, "Com ear plees."

"*Habla Espanol*, Señora?"

"*Muy pequeno.*"

"Very small, eh?" Jorge laughed, then began the routine questioning. "*Digame el appellido de su mama.*"

The American replied slowly. "I have three children."

"No, no. I mean the name of your mother, su mama."

"Tres."

"Señora, you have a mother?"

The American's delicately freckled cheeks flushed. "Si," she replied.

"Then write her name. *Escribalo.*" He handed her a pen. "Also your father's name."

Jorge was relieved to see that she understood.

"*Nacionalidad, Norteamericano*, no?" Was she married? What color was her skin? Pale white. The freckles on her nose fascinated Jorge. And should he write blond or brunette?

"Señora," he looked deliberately into her eyes, "*sus ojos*, what color?"

She squinted at him, the distance narrowing between her eyes. "*Azuel* or *verde?*" When she did not answer, he typed with one finger, 'hazel.'

"Do you read? Do you write?" When she did not reply, he wrote *Si*.

Lights in the room blinked and went dark. Chattering stopped. Everyone raised their eyes to the ceiling fan. The sound faded until the rotating arms finally came to a stop. The American glared at Jorge.

He rose from his chair. "Señores y señoras, I am very sorry, but everyone will have to wait for the electricity, maybe only a few minutes." (Or part of a day, as last week.) "I will check on the power outage."

Actually, he went to the Espresso Café down the street. When he returned to the Ministerios De Relaciones Interiores, most seats had emptied, but the American was still there. She sat grimly clutching her handbag. He smiled as much as to say, "There, dear, it is all right."

She leaned back in a chair, wiping her brow with a lace handkerchief, then took something from her handbag, unwrapped it, sticking a piece of gum in her mouth. Chewing like a dog on bone. Most undignified. Funny, those North Americans.

At exactly 11:45 the lights glowed. Jorge flicked the switch a few times and the flying machine slowly gained momentum. Checking his watch, he said to the few still seated, "Ladies and Gentlemen, I am very sorry, but it is too late to begin the photographs. Please come back *a las catorce.* Two o'clock."

There was grumbling and feet shuffling as those who had remained in the Ministerios De Relaciones Interiores rose from their chairs. Jorge thought he heard the American say, "Oh, this is impossible!"

~~~

As he knew she would be, the American was first at the door. Jorge turned the key in the lock and stepped back, motioning her to enter. He noticed fine beads of perspiration ringing her forehead. "Good afternoon, Señora!"

The fan was turning but it was hot inside, the hottest part of the day. Jorge managed to face the afternoon hours with the cheerful knowledge that they soon would be over. "Señora, I am very sorry, but the photographer is not here yet. You must wait."

By the time the photographer arrived, many people had filed back into the waiting room. Jorge processed their papers, matching correct photos with applications. He was careful because the new man, nephew of the mayor, had recently taken the job of photographer.
~~~

The American stood in line patiently until she was directed into a small dark room. When she came out she walked straight to Jorge shaking her head. "Nothing more?"

So, the American thought she was finished! "No Señora, *los dedos.* He held up his fingers and smiled. The American sat down.

Later, he motioned her to follow him to the back of the room. There at a high table with a naked light bulb hanging over it, a man placed applicants' fingers, one by one, onto a moist pad and pressed them onto the official paper. He did this over and over again. Jorge stood by, talking with a group of men while she waited. He enjoyed his role as protector of the woman at whom the men stared. Jorge raised his eyebrow at the man who took her hand, first the right hand and then the left, all of the fingers but one. The American held up her left thumb. "This, this!" she said.

"What?" asked Jorge, though, of course, he understood. He shook his head yes. Yes, he would help her, and he was just about to speak when the photographer called to him.

"No, is that so! The negatives are not good?" By his watch, the hour was 15:28. No, the photographer did not have time to get new film today.

Jorge returned to the American and said to his co-worker, "Do it, do the thumb print."

Her left thumb was pressed against the inkpad. The American appeared triumphant. She raised all ten spotted fingers before Jorge and smiled. He led her to a spattered grey wall basin. While she stood in line to wash her hands, he returned to his desk with her application.

When she finished scrubbing her fingers, she marched to the door and turned to Jorge with a quick smile. He called to her, "*Señora, momentico!* One moment, plees!"

Crossing the room, he spoke to her in his most confidential tone, "Señora, I am very sorry, but the *fotografía no es buena.* The negative is bad."

The American's mouth gaped and her eyes wrinkled together.

There! He knew he had caught her where he wanted her. Smiling his sympathetic smile and looking straight into the American's narrowed hazel eyes, he said in his best English, "You will have to come back tomorrow!"

MARCY

Marcy brushed wisps of moist hair from her forehead. It was hot, so hot! Sun turned the desert into thick haze so that all she could see distinctly through the car windshield was an oil pipeline that followed the highway and walking on top of the pipe, a goat looking as strangely out of place as she felt sometimes in her world contained within a patio wall and a refinery gate. But today, alone, she was going to the village.

She had come once before and hadn't returned. The village was hot and dirty. Sand blew into ruts on the roadway and scraps of paper spiraled into the air, floating down to be caught by wind and carried on. Children ran naked and pigs foraged at doorways. The smell of dried urine had made her ill. Today nothing seemed to have changed. Children, dogs, and chickens scurried in front of the car. She drove cautiously, waving children aside.

The sea suddenly shimmered into her eyes, hugging the shore like a mid-day celestial soup caught in a witches' cauldron and splashed to the rim by a deeply stirred ladle. Marcy pulled to the side of the road.

The cerulean sky was theatrical backdrop for huts near the water, each ochre casa trimmed in splashes of red, green, blue—with its own surprise of color and variation of a simple facade. Not far away was a dwelling, one layer of paint fading into the former in a mirage of dissolving colors and, where the mud-stucco crumbled, a wattle structure of sticks was bared.

At the open door, children toddled in and out. (She'd learned at Women's Club that often the children's stomachs were swollen from lack of food or an abundance of intestinal parasites.)

A woman came to the door. Her face had the look of fruit left too long in the sun. She called, "*Ven*, Pablito. Come!"

"Yes, Mama! Here I am."

"Where is Mariela?"

"With Marina."

"And where is Marina?"

"At the corner with Mariela."

"Then, Pablito, bring the water, now!" She placed two large buckets on a rod over the boy's shoulders and he ran off.

Other boys playing with the frame of a long-discarded folding cot passed in front of Marcy's car. "*Corre! Ven conmigo!* Run! Come with me!"

She thought how beautifully the melodic syllables of the Spanish language flowed from the mouths of children. Then another sound came to her, a wailing.

A child, in his excitement, tripped by the side of her car. With the hurt of a gashed knee he let no moan from his lips, but picked himself up, limping, and followed the capricious trail of his playmates.

"Are you all right, Chico?"

"It is nothing," he called. "Run! Run! Advance on the guerillas!"

A naked toddler came into view. He paused in the intensifying sunlight as if he were a bronzed cupid in a faraway garden. A slender girl followed him. She caught Marcy with her wide eyes, then hobbled away in a halting gait. Down the little girl went toward the bay—stumbling, falling, pulling herself up amidst obstacles of wood and refuse. There a man sat under a lean-to canvas, wood chips and logs scattered near the frame of the fishing boat that he was hewing by hand.

Again, Marcy heard a strange moaning. Then men's laughter rolled in waves off the water. A fishing boat bobbed some yards off shore, the mast swaying, gently fencing a few cumulus clouds. Perhaps, thought Marcy, this is the way men escape their womenfolk when the fishing season is over, days spent lolling on their boats. Flags were flying from the halyard. A celebration? But no, she saw that the flags were men's pants washed and hauled up to flap in the sea breeze.

Marcy had gone, once, out on the sea swells where king mackerel run. She had watched a fisherman standing in his boat throw a single handline, easing it out, then pulling it in with such grace that she thought of ballet, of an art form evolving from this practical act.

The people seemed to have an affinity with the moments of their lives that she felt she did not have, her life tangled in lines of ought and doubt, and fraught with possibilities that would or would not be realized.

She looked up as a young man playing a cuatro sauntered down the road, singing:

> *"Quisiera verte tan cerca*
>
> *– sentir tu boca…*
>
> *con ansia loca –"*

He stopped at the open car window. "Señora," he asked, "are you lost? I would be glad to help you. No? Then, have you trouble with the car?"

How could she say that she simply wanted to be in the village, and say it in Spanish, yet? How could she say that, just for this morning, she needed to look out on others to find herself? All she said was, *"No, gracias."*

Down the road the boy called Pablito was returning, laboring under the weight of the water buckets carried on his shoulders. "Mama!"

As the door opened, Marcy strained to see into the interior of the casa. What came in view were framed pictures of the Virgin Mary and Simón Bolívar astride his horse and, on a chair, an infant tied by a rope. The child had a piece of corn cake in his hand and was crying, though he made no effort to get out of the chair. His crying mingled with sounds from nearby huts and the sporadic strange moaning.

Beyond the corridor, sun shone into a patio where chickens pecked at pebbles and tomatoes grew in oil barrels. A woman took the child from the chair and set him in a basin, then picked up a can of water and poured it slowly over the infant's copper curls and brown shoulders. The child screeched in half cries of surprise and delight. And yet, other cries came to Marcy, disturbing her at intervals, like waves breaking on shore.

A girl came into the patio and carried the child away. The woman began washing clothes methodically in the basin. Above her bloomed a *frangipani,* the spiked leaves centered with fragrant white blossoms.

From across the road a woman called. "Petra! *Una hembra!* Yes, it was a girl, and old Carmela was there."

Suddenly the American understood. The moaning had been a woman in the throes of labor. Why did she, who had given birth and heard that cry in antiseptic hospitals, not recognize the sound when it flowed onto a sandy road from a hut in a fishing village?

The woman came from the patio and closed the door. Marcy felt something taken away, denied her. She drove past the huts in the village and followed the highway back to her tiled patio with its blooming frangipani, to her children and husband to whom the maid would be serving lunch.

BRIGGS

The automatic glass door hesitated before it swung into the main office of the refinery. In that second, Briggs wondered just what-the-hell he was doing here, anyway. Not that he hadn't wondered at other times in the last five years, but today the door annoyed him.

He walked across the terrazzo floor. On the wall was an aerial photograph of the refinery, which at mid-century was the largest in the world. Huge oil storage tanks were white dots against a grey mottling of rocks and sand. The great diamond-shaped voids of two fuel-oil pits edged into the desert and below the cliffs at the terminal, four supertankers, like pocket pens, floated in Amuay Bay. Briggs saw his house in the photo, the treelined streets of the town built by the oil company, Judibana, pride of Estado Falcon, a garden on the desert of Paraguaná.

But sometimes, he thought, why not pick up and go back to the U.S.A.? His head was ajar from the party last night. Too many scotch and cokes.

He walked down the hall, greeted by "Hola," *"Buenos dias… Good morning"* or "Say, Briggs…"

He walked past the two secretaries, glancing at the prettier one who was having an affair with his neighbor.

Briggs did not turn in at the door with his name on it but walked past all the doors along the hallway and out to the coffee shack. He would have coffee before facing whatever disasters, some in the form of blue complaint slips, might await him at his desk. He slipped coins from his pocket and gave them to the man behind the counter. The fellow struck Briggs as looking remarkably like Genghis Khan—eyes hard, uncompromising, forming a barrier between himself and polite conversation.

The steaming espresso was black as asphalt, hot as hell, and strong enough to make his hair stand up. But Briggs couldn't stomach it sweetened with teaspoons of sugar as the Venezuelans did.

"My change?" he asked. Genghis swept the territory with his black eyes and gave him a resistant stare. Briggs had learned to be careful. Not to be taken advantage of. Be easy and you are taken for a fool.

Office hours had begun fifteen minutes ago, but the courtyard was filled with men, casual in short sleeves, greeting him and one another, bracing against a morning breeze, chatting over their breakfast coffee and *pan dulce* roll, as if there were nothing else to do. On second thought, was there? Was he slipping, maybe heading for the booby hatch? He heard the word 'strike' floating around in conversations and that caught him up short. The theme came up periodically. He never liked it.

"Good morning, Briggs." One of the ambitious younger Americans who worked for him was at his elbow. "After that party last night, needing some coffee this morning?"

"Yes," he answered.

"Some party!" said the young American. It had been some party. His neighbor was caught kissing the secretary and one of the wives, slightly drunk and thinking she could tango, had slipped on the dance floor slick from a spilt daiquiri and sprained her ankle. The broiled *lomito* tenderloin was excellent and the stereo – Billos Caracas Boys – loud. The young man's wife was something of a celebrity at the party, standing on a chair, singing show tunes from Broadway.

The wife had come marching into his office last week with a policeman, demanding that he, Briggs, do something because she got arrested for driving without a license. She couldn't pass the driver's test in Spanish. The police were ready to put her husband in jail, as was customary, and the longer Briggs kept the police waiting, she said, "the higher the fine would be," and she wasn't going to pay the bribe.

The Company pays, the company always pays. Maybe Briggs was running one big welfare department. (God knows, jail was a rough place, but he could almost smile at the thought of the fellow behind bars, his tearful wife daily bringing him plates of food.)

As an American, Briggs was always on the spot to say the right thing, do the right thing, and how the hell did he know what that was? Briggs considered his half-empty cup.

"Have you seen *El Diario*?" asked the young man.

"Haven't been to my desk yet."

"Some party we're likely to have tonight if the 11 o'clock shift goes on strike!"

"Oh, God!" Briggs hated strikes. He didn't like to cross the lines, either. Twelve-hour shifts and his assignment was climbing up tanks to gauge oil for shipment. Something he wasn't anxious to do—he had a fear of heights. And the last time there had been a fire in the refinery, his wife had wakened him in the night to the sound of the siren – a fearful sound – three sharp blasts repeating and repeating. He had been so alarmed that he put his shoes on first, his best pair, then tried to pull up his pants in an awful struggle. When he arrived at the refinery, the fire was already under control.

Briggs knew that it was time for a vacation when things got on his nerves. Worry was a luxury that he couldn't afford. Not with the recent burning of a bus on the highway and the bombing of the pipeline from Maracaibo to the refinery. But tankers kept right on filling with crude. Not without a little sabotage. Too many valves could be turned or easily overlooked. Fifty thousand barrels loaded in a tanker, then discovery that the spec's were off and the crude had to be pumped back out. What a mess! He was glad he had an office job. But how many times had he decided to quit? Find a job back home while on his month's vacation?

"Hello, Briggs, some party last night!"

"Some party," he replied dutifully.

"Have you seen *El Diario*?"

"Not yet. What does the newspaper say?"

"You won't believe this, Briggs… shows how stupid…"

"You mean the strike?"

"No, a strike is about to happen most of the time. But yesterday, this guy climbs the radio tower to do some repair, then cuts all the guy wires holding up the tower. He falls, breaks his leg. Lucky it wasn't his neck! Broke the refinery's safety record. One hundred twenty-seven days."

"Well, remember Tex? Broke the best safety record yet, dropping a manhole cover on his toe."

"Yeh! Amazing the refinery runs at all. What will they do without us?"

"The revision, you mean? The Venezuelans will do all right," Briggs added. "The question isn't if the assets of the company go to Venezuela with the nationalization, but when."

"What about us, our jobs?"

Briggs, like all the foreigners, was concerned. With talk of nationalization there was a curious undercurrent of excitement. One waited expectantly for firecrackers to explode, even for one rainy day of thunder and lightning and damn the fires. He'd seen lightning ignite a storage tank and set oil burning.

On the way to his office, Briggs glanced into the printing room. *El Diario* was out for today, but once again, Briggs thought of the time when the revolution and the overthrow of the dictator had just begun.

He had recalled the details many times.

Briggs had returned to the office after a noon meal at home. He was sitting at his desk when someone pushed open the door. He looked up to see two strangers standing over him. His eyes riveted to shoulder holsters bulging from the men's suit jackets.

"Where is Jesus Rodriguez?" they demanded.

"I, ah, I don't know," he stammered, feeling a chill rise through his body. "I don't know." Jesus was the clerk who worked for Briggs, an easygoing young man who might come through the door at any moment.

"Don't you know where he is?" they asked.

"Maybe in the printing room," Briggs said weakly. As soon as he said it he wished he hadn't. The men left immediately.

He hoped against hope that Jesus wasn't there, but the secret police arrested him. But for what reason? The betrayal haunted Briggs for months. He told himself that he had been caught off-guard, that there was nothing that he could have done to prevent the arrest.

When the dictator was overthrown, when heroes were made and Admiral Wolfgang Larrazabal named President, Jesus came forward, a victor. He had printed inflammatory revolutionary pamphlets after hours in the refinery printing office. At the height of the fighting, Jesus was freed by revolutionary forces and eventually became something of a hero with his photo in the national newspaper. Jesus never came back to his job as clerk. He had 'made it' in the right political circles and was given a government job in Caracas.

Briggs admitted the guy had guts and willingness to risk all without weighing the consequences; fear behind him, emotions to the fore, fighting for a cause. Briggs admired that. He himself was too introspective, could easily doubt the necessity of action.

He opened the door to his office. There were the complaint slips on his desk, a strike notice in *El Diario*, and a plea for a job from a man whom he'd already refused. Union laws, incompetent workers, government. He'd had to fight them all. The social problems of the people, the extra problems they created for him, were not his responsibility. So why didn't he quit, just go home? Maybe, he thought, he really did care about the place.

Two Marias

The two Marias sat together eating their evening meal of black beans and arepa, scraping the freshly baked cakes of white cornmeal around their bowls, catching the beans on the arepa's toasty crust, thrusting bites into their mouths, slowly masticating, savoring their food.

The dark hair of Maria, the elder and aunt, usually worn in a coil at the nape of her neck, fell loosely, touching her bare feet as she sat on a low stool on the cement floor in the maid's room.

Young Maria, her face bovine, a thin dress pulled tight over her belly, sat on a cot, the worn coverlet mended and patched by the careful sewing of Maria the elder.

"Mia," asked the aunt, "did you eat an egg today?"

The girl nestled herself on the cot. "I asked the señora for an egg."

"I will get some oranges for you from the market, little niece. The oranges come very big from the mountains now. Without rain last year, the oranges were small and full of seeds. Everything grows better this year."

"Twice as big," said Mia, patting her stomach.

"Everything is plentiful but *la plata*, the cash, especially with you here, Mia. I would like to send you to the government clinic."

"I don't need to waste money to go to the clinic. I feel very well."

"At the clinic they give you tests of the blood, many tablets and injections. And a pill so that you won't make another baby right away."

"But the priest won't let me do that!"

"But he doesn't have the babies. You will learn how dearly babies cost! I carried four times, did you know that? I could not carry mine long enough. Someone said I had the evil eye on me, but God gave me my son at last, and today I say to him, 'My son, stop driving that taxi long enough to go to the dentist to get your rotten teeth pulled.' But he won't. A child will not listen to his mama, even when he is grown!"

"Maria!" The American señora was calling again. Maria the elder sucked the last of the beans and arepa from her fingertips, shaped her hair into a bun, tucked her feet into slippers, and pattered through the back entrance of the house into the kitchen. Maria had served the dinner guests and now it was time to clean the kitchen.

"Left a mess for you," said the señora, standing in the doorway to the formal dining area. Maria quickly assessed what was to be done. She heard laughter of dinner guests now retired to the patio. The American hesitated. She had a way of sighing, of weighing what she was going to say to Maria. "Maria, that girl has got to go!"

"She is my niece, Señora."

"Then tell her to go."

"She has no place to go."

"Well, she can't have a… Well, I suppose…"

Maria knew that the señora would not want her to quit. She needed her to buy the fish and vegetables off the truck. Maria was necessary because she knew very well English. Tomorrow she would ask for a slight raise in pay. She would set the money aside for the new expenses of a baby.

"Please clean the dining table, also," said the señora and, with that, she returned to the guests.

Maria put her attention to the disarray: pots and pans, napkins wadded and stained with jelly, debris littering the counters, broken bits of Parker House rolls that the señora had made, glassware standing on salad plates, expensive chunks of lettuce turning brown in salad oil, the señora's best chinaware at the counter's edge, wine glasses by a roasting pan, a half centimeter of grease in the pan.

A bombardment of priorities clicked in Maria's head as she revised the space in the kitchen, sectioning the stemware from cooking bowls, putting silverware to soak, never leaving it unsudsed, undried, but polished as best as only she could, until gleaming.

Maria took pride in the thoroughness with which she did her job. From the first garbage scraping to the last counter scrub, she took interest in each item, happy to discover the little pickle fork with tines spread like a broom and the sugar spoon with a windmill that actually turned and dessert spoons in pretty flower designs, each spoon different.

She took from the cupboard a common breakfast plate and saved a slice of leftover roast beef, a Parker House roll, and globs of butter and jam.

"Here, Mia, a little extra for you."

"I think the señora doesn't like me here."

"Why do you say that?"

"Because when I asked her this morning for an egg, she saw me take four pieces of toast, also."

"But the señora is not ungenerous."

"She saw the fingernail polish."

"What fingernail polish?"

Mia splayed ten unskillfully painted orange-red fingertips over her stomach.

"Why did you do that?"

"She has five bottles, anyhow."

"I've told you, Mia, not to go into the house. You are lucky the señora lets you stay here at all! You're not to go in there, do you understand?"

Mia nodded placidly, letting her fingers stray over her stomach, scratching gently.

"That dress doesn't fit you anymore. I have done all the mending I can. What are you going to do?"

"I don't know. The woman down the street sells baby clothes. I would like some, but I cannot let you pay for them."

"So you can pay?"

"Oh, no! I don't have any money, but I am sorry if you must pay for them. I would like some diapers too!"

"Better to have diapers where there is plenty of running water."

"When I go back to the mountain, I will miss the flushing toilet and the shower with hot water."

"You are going back to the *pueblo*, then?"

"I can't go now, Auntie, you know that—but when my baby comes, I want to go back."

"Back to that boy again?"

"Yes."

"But Mia, why do you think I brought you here?"

"Because Mama told me to leave!"

"Because that boy sits up there on the mountain at the Iscardo store smoking and drinking and enjoying talk about himself. He should be earning money to support you."

"And where can he find a job?"

"He could work the fields for his uncle."

"And where would the money come from that?"

"That's true. All I can remember of my childhood is cutting cane in the fields, working until I was exhausted. And always hungry! Pain clamped across my stomach at night on the long walk back up the mountain."

"Maybe, when he sees his pretty baby, who will look just like him, then everything will be all right."

"And how will you live, under a banana tree?"

"Maybe he will get a job."

"Ah, Mia, you are too young to understand! That boy will not stand by you."

"But I love him!"

The two Marias fell silent, scraping last morsels of food from their bowls. Maria the elder was thoughtful, figuring at what price she might buy a dress for Mia with her next week's raise. She would ask the señora again tomorrow. Maria the younger thought how pleasant the day when she would proudly hold her baby in her arms.

Together they rinsed their bowls in the bathroom basin in the maid's room and set them to dry on the window ledge by a half glass of water grown dusty, a bottle of orange-red nail polish, and a spool of thread with a rusty needle stuck in it.

Marisol

Young Marisol swings open the screened door, hops onto the grass, bird-like, black eyes bright, her tight braid-tail flopping at the hollow of her back. She turns to a western sun low over the sea, white ruffling of her blouse a mantle to bronzed skin washed by winds and polished by the sun.

Marisol, Mary of the Sun, *del sol*, claims birth as polished stone claims earth and nothing more. She tips her head. Listens for a rustle under fallen *almendra* leaves. Looks for claw-scraped almonds in dry grass blades.

She calls, "Where are you, little one? Pajarito!"

The bird, her young life's love, at morning escaped the small bird hut and now with household duties done, Marisol seeks the pajaro. But where is he? Does he not hear her call? Or listen to the splash, splash, splash of the sea's lace petticoats rushing to the shore?

She listens hard, her forehead broad, cheekbones high, wind-whisked strands of gold-red hair attesting to this day, ascendancy of Spanish conquerors over Andean terrain. They sought riches in vain, but her gold strands remain.

Marisol digs her toes in a bed of transported earth brought to desert stone. Stone ground by sand, ground by wind and surf. Flowers too, bright bobbing in the breeze, were flown in a bird of steel from some far land. Seeds brought to stone to plant a ring of brightness on the dull desert floor.

Marisol lifts a low branch of pink-blossomed oleander. No blinking pajaro is there. No movement but the billowing around her slender legs of a full-flowered skirt catching the oleander's bough as if to grow there too.

Marisol pulls the skirt, caught in sudden wind like sails at sea. Turns to meet sea's sparkling crescents shining in her eyes, sun-sent bangles, adornments of a lady fine whose heart is fluttering.

Does he not see, her little love, the blinking of the sea to meet his own? "Pajarito, look at me!"

She scurries to the backyard fence where washed clothes flap, wrapping around a line. Is he under lemon tree's bird-green leaves that weave a thorny path to fruit of bitter succulence? But no small bird sulks there in the branching, barbed enclosure.

Marisol steps onto crackling dried grass carpeting near a bed of periwinkles. Is he there? Her pajaro?

Shortly then, her love does come—chirping, crossing ground. From where? She sees that he is frightened now. Afraid that she will scold? The pajaro, round eye blinking, stares at her, white breast feathers ruffling above a yellow vest.

Marisol places a finger near his sharp-hooked bill. Will he accept the offering?

The bird hops near, raises one claw, then turns away.

"Come, little bird, come to me, Pajarito!"

Green ruffled feathers showing blue beneath short clipped wings, the bird turns one eye full to look at her. The moment comes. Parrot green, so small, is caught in her V-ed fingers brown.

"There my love, I have you now," sings Marisol. "Now you are caught and I am free!"

WALDO AND ERNESTO

Waldo looked at the luminous dial of his watch. Lights in the bungalow had gone out exactly twenty minutes ago. He and his brother, Ernesto, had waited, concealed in darkness and oleander in the residence camp where foreigners and engineers lived. Ernesto slipped out of his shirt and trousers, uncovering a black leotard which he had bought some months ago at a theatrical supply store in Caracas. Waldo opened a tin of black grease and applied it quickly to Ernesto's face.

The brothers were proficient athletes, wiry and muscled, perhaps driven to physical competence by their slight build, a fact that might be considered disadvantageous in other circumstances. Ernesto had bought an expensive pair of elevator shoes which he wore on special occasions when he wished his presence felt. But tonight Waldo put the shoes, along with Ernesto's clothes, into a sack which was strapped to his shoulders so that his arms remained free.

Precise measurements had been taken. The louvered glass window left an opening of twenty centimeters, wide enough to permit entrance of Ernesto's head when horizontal with the window ledge, that ledge being one meter seventeen centimeters from the ground.

Ernesto entered with little difficulty, head first, bent to the right, knowing that the bed was to the right of the window. Silently his shoulders slipped through. He was borne on Waldo's weight until his waist was inside the window and then he pulled his head to the right and touched one foot to the floor.

The wallet was within hand's reach. Also, a large gold coin necklace on the bureau. That was more than Ernesto had counted on. The couple lying on the bed did not move. He handed the wallet and necklace through the window to Waldo who was waiting, hands open. Waldo dropped the wallet and necklace into the sack and, as Ernesto leaned through the louvered opening, Waldo's powerful hands supported his descent from the window.

They listened a full minute, hearing nothing but palm fronds slashing at the wind. Then they moved to the next house.

All houses had the same floor plan. In each there was no pet dog, the head of the house slept in the same bedroom, and entry windows were sheltered by bushes or located away from the view of chance passersby. Tonight was chosen because only a sliver of moon shone through fast-moving clouds and it was the third workday of the month when men had cashed large paychecks and their wallets were full.

Again Waldo lifted Ernesto through a window. Again a wallet was in easy reach, but this time the wallet was in the pocket of pants draped over a chair, as Ernesto knew it would be.

Moving in darkness to the third house, they saw lights flash far off. Instinctively the men leapt ahead to a row of palm trees and stood motionless until the car had passed. Waldo checked his watch. He knew that, as on previous evenings, the patrol truck of the vigilantes, the refinery police, would not pass for another hour and fifteen minutes.

This house would give special pleasure. It was the house of the chief of police, head of the vigilantes. Ernesto had planned to rob it since the night a patrolman spied him inside the patio of an empty house and jumped from his truck to give chase. Ernesto made his escape, hiding for what seemed hours under a discarded packing crate.

Ernesto was ready now and anxious as they passed between houses, walking near bushes, concealing themselves as much as they could. No sight of anyone, no sounds. No house lights switched on, no baby cried out in the night.

The window was open as the others had been and again Ernesto passed through the louvered opening. He felt the quickening of his agility, the finesse of his movements. And this time he would do something that he had not spoken to Waldo about. The idea had occurred to him two nights ago while observing the house. The chief of the vigilantes and his wife had not yet arrived home when Ernesto stood at his post near a large hibiscus bush three meters from the bedroom window. He was awaiting their return and then a careful plotting of their habits in preparing for bed, when he heard a child's whimper that worked into loud cries until a voice, undoubtedly the maid's, said, "Pobrecita, poor little one, go to sleep."

A light had switched on in the second bedroom and Ernesto watched the maid hold the child, rocking her.

"Why do you cry so, my love?"

The maid had looked around the room and picked up a glass pig. Ernesto had seen such a pig once in a novelty store, amused at the custom of putting one's money in a glass pig in which coins could be seen. The maid shook the coins in the bank to quiet the child. The child stopped crying, sobbing only from time to time as the maid jangled the pig, accentuating the beat like maracas or tambourine.

Tonight, Ernesto would play a joke on the chief of police. He walked forward exactly eight steps and found the door to the child's room ajar. He opened it noiselessly with his elbow. His hand closed over the bank. He knew that his fine control could keep him from tipping the coins and causing possible calamity. A slight risk, but he must have the pig bank!

Waldo received the bank with some surprise, even impatience, but, because Ernesto took the greater risk, Waldo could not refuse. He wrapped the bank carefully in Ernesto's shirt. Then he heard a sound in the house. Had someone been disturbed? Had Ernesto made a fatal slip, over a pig bank? Inside, Ernesto stopped instantly at the movement of shrouded figures on the bed. He reached for the knife that was taped to his left forearm, just above the wrist. His fingers tightened on the knife handle.

Outside, Waldo waited. Finally Ernesto appeared at the window, a billfold between his teeth.

They waited by a bougainvillea. The houses were dark and vulnerable. The brothers swooped down like vultures for their last victim of the evening. Ernesto felt himself in good form. Under such conditions, he was pledged to the fulfillment of their plan, always glad to reach the last entry.

The louver needed a slight adjustment, then Waldo raised Ernesto's legs to the height of the window to support forward movement until he was able to pull his leg over the ledge. Success depended on Ernesto. But he was not moving!

Something unexpected had happened! The room had been rearranged and, as Ernesto pulled his leg through the window, he found himself on a bed. Suddenly a child sat up. Ernesto reached for the knife. The thought of the knife slicing warm flesh overwhelmed him, and then the child said, "Boy, you get out of here! I'll call my momma and daddy! Get out boy, you hear me now?"

Ernesto was confused. What was she saying? In that moment he turned and slipped out of the window and into Waldo's waiting arms.

Inside a light switched on. An adult voice said, "You go back to sleep now, hear?"

"But a boy was in my bed! His face was painted black!"

"It was only a dream, dear."

"But he put his feet on my bed!"

"Now, you go back to sleep! Goodnight!" The light was off. The door closed.

This time there was no waiting. Ernesto and Waldo fled. But as they rounded the corner of the house, thinking to make a break, they startled a burro nibbling at a patch of grass. The burro rendered a piercing bray that seemed to waken the world. Lights switched on again in the house.

Waldo and Ernesto ran, the indicting brays of the burro following them, altering the usual calm obscurity of night. Ernesto thought there was a flash of light behind them, but he didn't turn to confirm. They ran as fast as they could from bush to bush, leaping through open spaces, slipping from palm tree to palm tree, watching for a sudden flash of the vigilantes' truck heading straight for them.

Isabela

Isabela picked up the phone and dialed again the number that was so etched in her mind that it had become the automatic function of her fingertips and, as she waited for the ringing to cease, her long, polished nails tapped restlessly on the headpiece.

"*Hola? Hola? Esta Carlos?* Carlos is not there? When does he arrive? You don't know? *Si, si… gracias.*"

Isabela sighed and hung the phone back on the receiver. She wanted to cry aloud, but, because the señora was there, sitting at the table, she only whispered inaudibly to herself, "*El Dios sabe!* God knows!"

She returned to the dining table, to her pupil, the señora Americana, to the Spanish lesson and her still-steaming demitasse of café. She knew the American's gaze was on her and she felt the mask that was her face – an attractive face she knew, lightly powdered, with delicately curved nostrils and a slight indentation above silver-pink lips – she felt that face, like porcelain cracking from the corners of her mouth, about to shatter.

"Isabela, is something the matter?"

"No, Señora. Nothing important," yet her lips pressed hard against her teeth, forcing self-control.

"Then, do you take cream or sugar?"

"A little sugar, *por favor.*" A little sugar for my bitter heart, she thought.

"Isabela, I have a question before we begin the lesson."

"Yes, Señora?" She looked to her pupil as a friend. With an ear for Spanish, the American was quick to learn and quick to judge.

"How do you say, 'It is my turn'? I have to tell a neighbor that it is my turn to take the children to school next week. Somehow, it does not translate."

"You say *'Me toca a mí!'* Now, thought Isabela, me toca! *Mal suerte!* Bad luck! She turned to her pupil.

"Ah, Señora, life is hard. But life is much better for you North American women. You have good husbands, healthy children, money, everything!" Isabela sipped her coffee, unable to savor it. "I am not one of the privileged class, Señora. My father had not much money. He gained, then lost it under dictators."

"In the United States I am not considered rich. We Americans seem rich, here, because the poor are very poor."

"Los Pobres! Do you know that every day in the village there are people who have no money for food for their children? And prices go up because most food is imported. Life is not so difficult, if you have money!"

"Money is not happiness, it is not everything!"

"Perhaps not, but to the poor it is."

"Yes, Isabela, the poor suffer very much. But you are educated and know the world."

"Perhaps it seems so, but I know how bad things can be in our country, and it gives one to feel – how can I say – it is like drinking strong wine, the burning sensation is heavy inside oneself. We in this country have thirst for many things."

Isabela saw the señora observing her, watching her intently, as North Americans do, because it is easier to understand another language when one watches carefully the person speaking. But there was something more.

She had used the word 'class' when she talked of the beauty of cultured Latin women. They had talked of many things—of history and literature and articles on *la cultura* of Venezuela. The American told her that she and others like her were Latin America's hope for the future.

And Carlos had told her that too! How ardent his enthusiasm! He told her that she would be part of the future, a teacher who could influence minds. He had talked to her of a new freedom, a new future and that was why… but Isabela did not want to think of it. The señora was saying, "Yes, your country has great possibilities, and the first necessity is education for all the people. Then you will have true democracy."

How simple it all seems to the Americans! "Ah, but Señora, one can have democracy only where there is peace. When there is unrest, one must have control over people, or it is terrible!"

"But isn't it terrible to live under a dictator?"

"Yes. In truth, the people suffered much under the dictator, but when people had fear of the government they were also afraid to do bad things. However, there was always resistance. I remember street fighting in front of my father's house in Caracas when I was a girl. A bullet came through the window into the room where I was standing. I was so frightened. It was bad under the dictator. The people have suffered very much, from the time of the cruel Spanish conquistadores."

Isabela continued, "At the time of the revolution in 1958, my younger brother was sitting in a movie when the secret police entered and ordered all the boys into the army, and they forced them into cars and drove them to Caracas without letting families know. My father was frantic, not knowing where my brother was. Well, they stripped the boys of their clothing and put them in army uniforms to fight for the dictator right then and there. The boys had never shot guns, because guns were outlawed, and they were forced to fight for the dictator. Imagine why the troops were not loyal! Fortunately, my brother was 'okay,' but not one of the secret police was alive at the end."

"The revolution brought great hopes to Venezuela," said the señora. "I waved at truckloads of people shouting, waving flags, celebrating the overthrow of the dictator, Perez Jimenez. The feeling, what do you say? I know it is not 'catching' as we say."

"*Excitante.*"

"But what has happened since?"

"Elections and democracy. Even now, after the revolution, many things happen. Some good, some bad."

"I think eventually Americans will have to leave."

"No, Señora, you make more jobs and more money." Money! And what was she, Isabela, going to do? She reached for the demitasse and sipped the last of the warm sweet coffee. And now, she thought, must I drink only of the cup of sorrow? I am too young for this! She turned to the señora and said, "Yes, the poor in this country need many things."

"More coffee, Isabela?"

"No, gracias, Señora." Isabela realized then that she was tapping her fingertips noisily against the empty cup, an outward manifestation of her inner agitation.

"With us, Señora, it is not the same as with you. You are equal to men. You have rights. You live well. Señora, you don't know" - Isabela paused, realizing that she was slipping from the merely friendly into the familiar Spanish tense - "*tu no sabes*, you do not know how women in this country suffer. Do you understand?"

"But you are attractive, Isabela, and well educated."

The señora did not understand. Often Americans looked only at the outside, the facade of things.

The American continued. "A Latin woman knows that she is a woman, in a way North Americans don't. Perhaps it is the men!"

"Yes, the men! They give their attention to the women, yes, but I was going with a man a few years older than myself. I liked him very much. After all, I am twenty-four and that is old, to be *soltera*, a bachelor girl. The man I was going with was, what do you say, well read? He had interest in cultural things as I have."

"This man asked me to marry him and I was very happy. We were to be married when my father found out – how I do not know – that my fiancé already had children by another woman and was supporting them. My father was furious and immediately broke off the engagement and told my fiancé never to come near me again, or he would kill him. I think he meant it."

"Oh, Isabela!"

"I was heartbroken, but my father told me that had I married the man, I probably would have had to take care of those children when I would have plenty of my own." Isabela's voice softened. "I don't think I would have cared. You see, I loved the man. But I have never seen him since the day my father threatened him."

"It is true that your fiancé lied to you, or at least, did not tell you about the children."

"But, the men, they are *artero, entiende?* Cunning."

"Not all," said the señora, "and sometimes it is hard to know what is true. Reality can be a hard truth to learn! Isabela, was that your fiancé you called on the phone?"

"No. I don't know where he is, but I hoped to see him again. You see, after my father forbid the man to come back, I felt so sad that I could no longer stay with my father. I got a job in the school, *el colegio*. It is a good teaching job, no? I live now with my brother and his wife. They have been good to me." (But dios, my brother will kill me!)

"You know, Señora, it is custom that my brother is very strict with me. I can't go out in the evening to a movie, or anywhere alone. Always

I must go with him, or not at all. Señora, I am young. I do not like to be shut up all the time. I like very much to dance. But my brother never lets me out of his sight.”

“Perhaps North American girls have too much freedom.”

“I would like to be married, have a home and children.”

“But you are young and intelligent, Isabela.”

“But I am *soltera*, alone.” Could the señora see the agitation under the shell of her face? She continued quickly, “Because my brother would not let me meet anyone, I saw Carlos at school. He liked me right away and we talked very much. We saw each other there until the hour I had to be in the house. I was enchanted by Carlos. *Encantada.* What do you say? Lose your head?” Isabela sighed darkly. “I think that is very funny… I cared for Carlos and the way he talked. I was drawn to him through his ideas. It is easy to be fooled by such men!”

Isabela sat quietly for a moment, pondering whether to speak more to the señora. She felt a great bubbling of emotion inside her, pressing hard against the dam of her usual self-assurance. She was on the verge of shattering in a deluge of hot tears, a declaration of defeat which she did not wish to make. Isabela knew her weakness and how it betrayed her. She might not be able to control a torrent of tears. Instead, she brushed her hair back with her hands. “But excuse me, I am forgetting your lesson. Where are we?”

“This article from the daily paper.”

“Ah, *los comunistas!* They grow in numbers. They are even in the village. They give many promises and the people listen… Here it says: the head of the Central Committee of the Congress of the Communist Party declared that when the congress next convenes, they will be in power. It frightens me, because this will mean another revolution. Always unrest. But now it is not just the people, but outsiders.”

“Perhaps we Americans talk too much about communism.”

“No, it is a grave problem here. Carlos, he is on the teaching staff of the school, or was.” (It seems that he no longer answers the phone.) “He told me that the situation in Venezuela has changed very much.

That there is a *gran arrastre* of youth to communism."

"What is that word?"

"A great attraction, a movement of youth in universities and the high schools. Ah, Carlos talks a lot. He talks of national and international situations. He talks of transfusions of new blood into the country, the patriots of Nationalismo Revolucionario, a new order of government, freedom under the State. Words, always impressive words. The whole country is impregnated with lies by men like Carlos!"

How passively she had listened. "A new kind of freedom," he had said. She ought to be free to do as she pleased. Not freedom as in the past, only for the privileged few, but for all who now lived in servitude. Wasn't this what she wanted? She had believed Carlos. And now, because of him, she was in greater servitude and without freedom at all—at least for a while.

Isabela continued, not realizing that she was speaking, "And all those things he said! But he doesn't care for me. He won't even answer the telephone!"

"You love him then?" asked the señora.

"Carlos? Ah, Señora, I loved him! He took the best from me, and now he has left me."

"Nothing is as bad as you think."

"No, it is worse! I loved him too much. I am *encinta*. Pregnant!"

"Oh, Isabela—what will you do?"

"I don't know! Soon my brother will find out. You already can see, no?" Isabela stood up quickly. Her blouse hung loosely over her skirt.

"It is not the baby; that happens. It is Carlos! A baby should have a father to love it, you know. That is how I feel. The trouble is that now I am without a man. Soon I won't be able to work and then how can I pay for things? I spend money for injections every day at the pharmacy to keep from getting sick in the morning."

"What about your family?"

"My brother will throw me out. Dios, he will kill me! I don't know, maybe he will help me. He has children of his own."

"What about your father?"

"I left home very mad at him. You see, if my father hadn't threatened my fiancé, things would be different."

"But they aren't, Isabela."

"It isn't so much being pregnant, but I am angry. Very angry. First at my father, and then, my brother will be mad at me. And Carlos? He won't have me now! You see, he has taken my love and now he has left me! How could I love a person like that?"

"Isabela, may I give you advice? The next months will pass, then you can start teaching again."

"And who will take care of the baby? I have no mother or grandmother to take it."

"You wouldn't give the baby up?"

"No, never. I don't know... the trouble is, I am alone. Ah, I am so angry! And the whole Spanish lesson I have been talking so! I am sorry!"

"No, Isabela, I am sorry for you."

"Ah, Señora, the life of a woman, una mujer, is very hard, no? But *permitame*, the telephone?"

Isabela dialed the number again, her lips quivering as she waited for the ringing to stop.

"Hola? Hola! Esta Carlos?" There was no answer.

THE PAINTERS

Roofs of tile and newer ones of aluminum slope toward the road. A shutter bangs, a woman's face appears at a barred window. Rosita, the little seamstress, waits for her Federico to come home. She looks down the street, then disappears into the dark interior of her house.

Dogs bark and children shout, "Here they come!"

A bevy of children scurry before a station wagon that honks and bounces, raising waves of dust. The car stops abruptly near the church and two faces, masked in dark glasses and head scarves, get out of the car. The tall North American carries a pad of paper, a pen, and a bottle of ink hooked in long fingers. The other American grapples with a big wooden board, a box, and a folding chair. She wears pants like a man. After a few greetings, the women settle themselves and begin to draw and paint.

"Señora, see me!" The children plead, vying for position in front of the painters.

"QUIET! Quiet!"

"Shh!" chorus the children.

Dominico of the worker's syndicate glowers in a doorway, his impression heightened by the shiny black bathrobe he wears. "What is going on?"

"The painters!"

"But why do you think they come here? The rich gawk at our houses and they say 'ah,' and peek in the doors, but they do not know what it is to live here."

"Look, she draws *La Negrita!*" The North American's hand moves in intricate swirls that become a ring of tight curls.

Old Pedro comes slowly to watch. Perhaps the artist has caught those round eyes so darkly framed. What are the words when the poet asks, *"Porque no les pintan los angelitos negros?* Why don't they paint black angels?"

He looks at other girls with single long braids, pride of their Indian and Spanish blood. Suddenly La Negrita runs away. Other girls come close to the painters. "Draw me, draw me first!" "See my baby sister so pretty in my arms!"

The North American draws face after face—some smiling, others large-eyed and sorrowful; young girls with full faces or high-boned cheeks, in worn dresses too small or too large, boys in baggy cut-off pants.

"See! She draws Marina!"

"No! No! It's me!"

Each portrait creates the likeness and villagers nod approvingly. "Si, Señora, the drawing is equal, *es igual!*"

A cola truck, bouncing over potholes, comes to a sudden clamorous halt. Children flutter off the street and onto the curb of the plaza. Directly in front of the truck sits the painter who, with a few flourishes of her brush, stands, folds the campstool, and moves aside for the truck to pass.

Salas, the little policeman, strides forward, a pistol in a holster strapped to his grey uniform. "What's going on?"

Children teeter at the side of the road. Salas squints at the silent crowd, nodding, trying to give the impression that he is managing the situation—whatever it is.

A voice floats down the road.

"Federico again!"

"Isn't he always…"

"Borracho!"

"Drunk at this hour!"

Federico holds his cuatro like a baby and, as he approaches, he strums, singing:

"I wish to see you near…"

He rolls his dark eyes and the children shout gleefully and set to imitating their village buffoon. "The ear, Federico, the ear!"

Federico rolls his eyes again and stands transfixed in the center of the children. His right ear twitches.

"*¡Ole!*" shouts young Chico. He cuffs Federico and Federico steps back, raising his cuatro to fend off blows. As they box, Chico backs Federico onto the plaza where suddenly he sinks backward, his head coming to rest on the painter's lap. "*¡Ole!*" shouts the crowd.

Federico rises slowly and turns to the woman, "Pardon me, Señora, but it is my pleasure!" He bows and begins strumming:

"Quisiera verte tan cerca

sentir tu boca en mí boca

besar con ansia loca

y darte mí corazón."

"I wish to see you near…

to feel your lips on mine

to kiss with mad desire

and give to you my heart."

Perhaps the American smiled, but she started painting again.

"Señora, I have interest in art."

"Shuu! She understands what you say."

"The American?"

"Shuu!" caution the children. They point to Federico's house. Rosita leans against the door. Federico shrugs, crosses Calle Zamuro dragging his cuatro like a lagging child behind him. Onlookers move to the other side of the plaza and stand near the painter who perches on a campstool as if a twittering bird, flashing brushes and splashing bright colors across a white paper.

"What is that?"

"A fly on her nose."

Gonzalez, the lottery seller, waves slips over the crowd. "Here is the running sheet. Today is your lucky day! Win today!"

"Gonzalez, I'm betting on that fly this morning." The crowd watches a fly crawl in a circle at the tip of the artist's nose.

"She will shake her head."

"No, she will scratch."

"It is a long shot to bet on the North American."

"If she could see it, she'd draw it!"

The fly circles her dark glasses.

"Ayee! Do you all need American curiosities to entertain you?" The voice of La Loca descends on the crowd. "Are you so rich like them that you don't need to work? Lazy dogs! I say you ought not be out in the noonday sun. It gives one sun madness. Look to your own business. Do something today to be better off tomorrow or tomorrow is the same as yesterday. You waste time if you think those flowers smell sweet. Heed the wise, I say, don't watch the weak, though there is money in it for one who is wise, not lazy like you!"

La Loca's black mourning dress whishes after her, her last words incomprehensible, lost in gusts of wind on Calle Zamuro.

Old Pedro wished no dealing with her. Evil spirits come to her house they say, and she performs acts of curing that cost as much as a special mass. Padre Ignacio warned against La Loca.

"Look!" someone says. "The fly is gone!"

The painters stand up. Children clamor, asking to carry stools and paints to the car. "See, Señora, I can help!"

"*Adiós!*"

"*Hasta luego, muchachos!* Until next time."

Boys and dogs run after the car and into the dust from its tracks. The sun is now directly overhead, flooding the plaza, emblazoning the bust of Simón Bolívar. Pedro nods to El General and saunters back to his hut to eat his pat of arepa, to sleep all afternoon in his hammock, and to come out on the street to sit by his door when the sun is low and soothing breezes of evening bathe Calle Zamuro.

La Loca

Never before had the boy, Enrique, dared to scale the wall, to risk broken bottles cemented on top and cross a corner of the tile roof. As he jumped down into the courtyard, pebbles scraped against his feet, the sound magnifying in his ears, reverberating at La Loca's door, a sound that might bring someone to the discovery of him crouching behind an oil barrel.

It was dark. Enrique had broken the silence and now strange sounds came to him: palm fronds swishing like La Loca's skirts, the clang of a cooking pot, a squeak, as if an animal were trapped under the foot of a chair, and a thumping sound that pounded against his ribs like a marimba.

In the dark, herbs leaned out to touch him. The *Mata de Zabila?* The magic herb? His grandmother sometimes sent him into the village delivering her broths to the sick. Tonight a magic potent was drawing him to La Loca's door. He knew she was there, flickering in candlelight, staring at him through the wall, making him tremble.

He had heard of people cured, curses taken away, La Loca's long fingers pulling the evil out. When he looked through the door, he saw! Saw the magic. Enrique blinked. Something spun on the floor, like a pinwheel in the wind. Enrique pressed his eyes shut, then looked. A man was spinning on the floor in a vise-grip, knees to his chin.

"May the devil have mercy! *Merceeeed!*" Voices swirled about him. A girl sprawling in a shadowy corner rocked from side to side holding her belly, crying, "*Bruja*, let go of me!"

A hand of ice passed over Enrique's forehead. Candles flickered, then dimmed. A sour smell lodged in bubbles in his throat, made him grab his stomach. But he had seen La Loca's form rise from the altar and a picture there that he could not see in the glare of a candle.

La Loca raised something from the altar, passed it over the candle flame, and put it in her mouth. She passed a rag over the fire until it burst into flame and then trailed the smoke over the quivering body on the floor. The smoke turned thick and nauseous and for a moment Enrique thought he would either cough or gag and then be discovered, cursed, and surely chased away. He steadied himself against the wall. When he felt his head come back to his body, the convulsing sounds had quieted.

On the altar he now saw a picture of Maria Lionza flickering into life, the beautiful queen of jaguars and magic curers who looked, he was sure, straight at him.

"Go, demon! Go!" cried La Loca.

"This is the curse of my wretched wife," said the man, trying to stand. "She went crazy—when I got child with the girl. She did this to punish me!"

The girl crawled toward La Loca, "I begged her to give him up. Instead that witch-woman put this curse on me!"

"The ven – vengeance started…" said the man, unsteadily, "when I approached the house of my wife – a terrible crisis of nerves overcame me. I began running around, falling down, a hundred *cucarachas* crawling on me. I went to the girl's house, half mad with the cockroaches. The girl was already under my wife's enchantment – falling to the ground, screaming – and I fell in a spell right then – for I remember nothing but flames passing before my eyes."

"I went to fetch some water," said a woman crouching on the floor, "when I came upon the two of them in such a state, in an instant I felt outside my skin. I poured water on them – which didn't help – then I went, I don't know how, to a neighbor who has a truck. I knew that I had to get them as far away as I could from the jealous bruja who had put a curse on them. Then I lost my senses."

La Loca stood over the afflicted ones saying, "Demon, your power is broken!"

There was a sharp crack as if bones split. Then she stood before the altar, arms upraised. "Girl, you are cured. Do you acknowledge that you are free of the enchantment?"

"Yes, *Espiritista*, I'm cured!"

"Yes," said the man, "but I am not free of my wife. I am cured, but I am not free of her jealousy!" At that moment the girl screamed, fell on her back, and lay silent. The man fell over her. La Loca came toward them—toward Enrique in the doorway.

He jumped back, hit his knee on an oil barrel, then ducked behind it. La Loca stood at the doorway, her arms on the doorframe, stretching her long body, the candlelight casting her presence far into the darkness.

As soon as he could, Enrique fled over the wall.

~~~

He sat in the sun by his grandmother's hut, rubbing a cut on his foot, staring down the street at the dwellings on Calle Zamuro, finding her house there, as it always was, hex signs on the wall and broken bottles on top, one side of the double door painted black, the other red and no window facing the street. Vultures on the roof peak rested one claw and then the other, waiting.

"Enrique! Enrique!"

That was Emilita, Enrique's half-sister calling. He came around on the far side of the hut. Emilita stood at Grandmother's door, hands on her hips, looking mean, her bumps showing through the thin pink dress, yellowed at the armpits and smelling of sweat.
~~~

"Enrique, where have you been? What have you been doing?" Emilita didn't wait for an explanation. She never did. He was glad for that. "Grandmother sends you to the market for soap. Right now! I am washing clothes. Lazy boy! Have you seen anyone pass on the street? Of course not! You don't know anything!"

Emilita talked always in her sing-song voice. But why talk to this stupid half-sister? She was the one who knew nothing. Nobody knew what he had seen last night.

She gave him a coin. "Bring back change or I will hit you!"

Enrique tried to see beyond La Loca's door through a crack, her shadow passing, the same one that passed so quickly on the street – like the *tijeras*, the scissor-tailed birds gliding against the sky, cutting down sharply on the wind – but the door was closed.

He ran to get the soap, limping slightly for the cut on his foot. People were gathered inside the dark store, as though everyone was hiding from the sun. He walked past brooms, pots and pans, tin cups, and bottles of purple disinfectant. As he reached for a speckled chunk of blue wash soap, someone said, "What happened last night at La Loca's?"

"Do you know?"

Enrique felt a chill in his bones.

"They say she can pull the sickness out."

"La Loca was the cause of the disturbance."

"Not at all. She cured my aunt of the bronchitis she'd had for a year."

"The police have brought a detective."

"A detective? What for?"

Enrique dropped the blue soap and his coin on the counter. Everyone stared at him.

"Enrique, *que tal?* What goes?"

"Don't you want anything else?" asked the storekeeper. Usually

Enrique wanted pan dulce, a yellow bun with a sugary crust. He would buy one if he thought Emilita wouldn't notice the difference in change. But today the insides of his stomach were glued together. He wasn't hungry.

"Boy, are you all right?" asked the storekeeper.

"I have a stomach ache," he answered.

"Drink some sweet tea, then," said a neighbor. "It chases the upset away."

Enrique hated sweet tea. He turned from the counter as someone said, "I heard they found the remains."

Enrique's heart bolted out of his chest. The jealous bruja had got revenge!

"They say the vultures came."

"You're pale, Enrique," exclaimed the storekeeper. Enrique took his change and hurried from the store.

He returned to his grandmother's wall to wait for La Loca. And hardly had he sat down on the hard ground when the magic was on him. He shivered, though the sun was hot. Sight of La Loca's double-hinged door had made him tremble like jingle bells, *cascabels.*

She surprised him, appearing at her door, pulling at the black robe on her arms as if readying for flight. She came rapidly down the street, heading toward Enrique. A rope tightened around his stomach. What happened last night was pulling her to him.

Then he saw Salas, the policeman, and another man walking toward her. Did anyone know that he was at La Loca's last night? Had she seen him climbing over the wall? Would they arrest La Loca? Maybe put him in jail? Enrique jumped up to hide, but the men in passing only said to her, "Buenos dias!"

La Loca walked on toward him, her arms raised, her coat licking sudden gusts of wind, and when she turned toward Enrique, she looked straight through him—as if he wasn't there. He knew that was part of the magic, and he knew where that baby was now—circling overhead. The vultures had snatched it away and now it soared up there on dark wings, gliding, touching the sky.

THE ABRAZO

"Barbara, come here a moment?"

Barbara set the mop aside. The strong scent of pine oil rose from the terrazzo floor. *"Como quiera, Señora.* As you wish."

She adjusted the uniform which now strained across her stomach in the sixth month of pregnancy, and walked down the hall of an almost empty house. The señora for whom she worked was going back to the United States.

"Yes, Señora?" The American stood by the bed, the only piece of furniture not yet sold or packed away. She smiled at Barbara, not the easy smile to which Barbara had grown accustomed, nor the smile of the señora on the day Barbara had married in the church in the village, or the smile of understanding that passed between them many times, transcending barriers of language, but a smile that today was uneasy.

"Yes, Señora, what do you wish?"

"Could you use this?" The señora held up a baby's sunsuit embroidered with yellow ducks waddling toward a butterfly. "And this baby bonnet?"

"Thank you, yes, Señora."

When Barbara had mopped all the floors, washed the last few dishes, hung the last clothes to dry in the wind, she showered for the last time under the hot and cold water. She checked to be sure that she had left none of her belongings in the maid's quarter and carried a wicker basket with a sack of clothes, an iron skillet wrapped in newspaper, and a large cracker tin.

The señora opened the car door and Barbara pushed the basket onto the back seat, then seated herself in front with the señora.

"For all the things, many thanks."

"For nothing, Barbara. I don't need them now."

The American drove through the streets of the oil camp, past the company school where Spanish and English flowed equally from the classrooms, past rows of stucco homes with walls shielding patios from the wind and sun of Paraguaná. The American drove to a bus stop.

"Señora, I cannot thank you enough for the cooking pan, the tin for storing food – you know the fight with roaches – and the basket will be fine to put my baby in, when it comes."

"Do you know, Barbara, that all my children slept in that basket when they were babies, until they were touching head and toe at either end. And, I slept in it too, when I was a baby."

"In truth, Señora?"

Barbara glanced at the señora. Their eyes caught for a moment. She knew that the señora had seen in her face the common fear that even now was creeping into her heart. "Now I have my first baby, but it is too soon. It is not good to have too many babies. I wish for only two children, or perhaps three. Some Americans from the camp came to the village to talk to the women about birth control and then a priest was sent from the city and he told us we must not break the laws of the church. But in truth, Señora, the old priest doesn't know anything about having children or how it is not to have food for one's child. I think our own Padre Ignacio will help us, but he must be careful or displease his superiors."

"Can you get help from a doctor at the clinic?"

"Yes, Señora, but what shall I tell the padre?"

"Just how you feel, exactly. I wish you luck!"

"Yes, Señora. Here is the corner."

"Is it time for the bus to arrive?"

"What hour is it now?"

"Eleven forty-five."

"The bus should come in a little while. But one can never be sure."

"Then I will park here. It is too hot to stand in the sun."

"I will miss you and your children, Señora."

"It has been a pleasure to have you with us, Barbara. I couldn't have managed the parties, the dinners, without your help!"

"For me it has been much more. Do you know, very soon after we married, my husband lost his job? We got married because he had the job. I could get a job, but he could not. Do you know, we paid each month fifty bolivars rent for a little house, even when a small package of rice costs a bolivar. When he lost his job my husband started building a house, cement block by block. My pay this week will buy the door. It is a necessity because the neighbor's goats go inside and boys urinate on the walls. Now I can get the door to keep them out."

"I don't see the bus coming."

"Sometimes it is late."

"Barbara, do you remember the first day you came to work for me?"

"Si! I was just pregnant and I tripped and fell."

"And I sent you home to rest. I knew that the fall frightened and hurt you, and I was afraid that you might have the authorities come and try to sue me or bribe me."

"But, Señora, it was I who was afraid that you might dismiss me, falling down on my first day of work!"

"But I didn't, did I?" The señora smiled, then the smile broke as if touched by lemon. She turned away and looked far down the road.

"I wish you happiness, Señora."

"Thank you, Barbara, but we must leave. And what will you do now?"

"After the baby comes, I will get a job again, here in the camp."

The two women were silent a moment, the Venezuelan and the American, sitting together in the car. Then the señora turned to Barbara. "Life is strange, isn't it? I've often thought how easily we might have changed places."

"Oh no, Señora!"

"But we have the same *sentimientos*, the same feelings for things."

"Yes, I have felt this too. Oh! The bus comes now. Have a good trip to the United States, Señora!"

"Thank you, Barbara. I wish you good luck! Here, let me help you with the basket."

They hurried from the car to the bus stop. The bus approached like a giant blue loaf of bread—rumbling, rolling forward on the flat desert road.

The two women embraced, touching cheeks, patting each other on the back in the traditional abrazo. "Good-bye, Barbara!"

"Adios, Señora!"

The American handed the basket to Barbara as she climbed onto the bus. The door clanked shut. Barbara set the basket on the bus seat and heard a woman near her say, "You shouldn't be so friendly with that North American."

"She is leaving, anyway."

"That is good! Better the foreigners go!"

As the bus rolled on, Barbara turned, eyes blurring, to see the American raise her hand in a last parting gesture.

The Eight O'Clock Hour

Perhaps she might have had time to decide properly if she had read the note before leaving the hotel, but in the rush of a taxi speeding down the curling *autopista* that in Latin frenzy carried traffic out of the valley of Caracas, over the mountains to the seaside port, she had forgotten to open the envelope.

At the hotel, Janet had returned her key to the desk and asked for any messages. In the past week she had received many notes, some from children in her third grade class.

"Dear Señorita: Have a good trip." "Please come back." And from the child who, with lovable impishness, had given her the most trouble in class, a simple note, *"Te Amo.* I love you." That almost made her cry. But Janet took pride in her ability to keep a level head, to never let emotions override her good sense.

The letters were packed in a suitcase, all but the note picked up at the last moment at the hotel, handwriting on the envelope not recognized, the note forgotten until she was at the airport ready to board her flight.

An air of expectancy, of arrival and departure, billowed through the waiting room: voices of stylishly dressed señoritas and men in dark business suits, masses of humanity, speaking multi-languages, all ears tuned to the drone and screech of arriving and departing planes, and a female voice that cut through space and time to announce Janet's flight to Miami.

She remembered the note in her purse, tore open the seal, and read: "You are not leaving! Please wait. Hotel Macuto, a las 20.00." (Eight o'clock this evening!) "Yours forever, Juan."

Janet was thrown into a panic. He did care! No time to think!

The moment was now – to decide – and she had so little on which to decide so much! Yes, that was it! She could always take another flight. She went to the counter and insisted that her luggage be retrieved. The agent argued with her. "Are you sure you want to do this, Señorita?"

"Yes, of course!" she replied sharply, but her heart said, are you sure you want to do this, Janet? It was not at all what she had intended. But there was Juan's note. "You are not leaving!" She was sure it was an exclamation point and not a question that he had written so hastily.

"I've got time, plenty of time," she had repeated to herself in the taxi that took her from the airport by the sea to the tree-lined streets of Old Macuto and the hotel he indicated.

She was deposited there in a dark room with three pieces of luggage. Janet shifted them methodically into order, but her mind was in disarray. She could not sort priorities. The sea had suddenly changed and she was floating erratically, a rudder lost, her course altered and she did not know why... exactly.

She knew that in the past year she had carried secret thoughts of Juan, had been infatuated with him, even, but her friends had said, "Janet, take care for that Juan—he is a charmer, a 'ladies' man.'" And she had kept a level eye with him. But what could he see in her? She had no illusions of herself as a beauty. Standing with her Latin girlfriends, dressed for a party, they with their vibrant coloring and bright dresses glamorously cut and silver-pink smiles; Janet, with her mouse-colored hair, her too-pointed chin, and that "scrubbed-behind-the-ears" American look—alongside them she felt simple and dull.

"Watch out for that Juan," they said. "He is a handsome one and a good catch, but he likes the women." Yet, hadn't she been flattered that he even noticed her?

"Am I going absolutely daffy? What am I doing here?" she said aloud. Then she panicked. Who was Juan? What had he said to her? What did his voice sound like? Times they had been together were crowded with other people, at parties, light talk and laughter. Sometimes he had picked up a guitar to sing and she told herself that she only imagined he was singing the silly, romantic words for her—at least, what she could make of the Spanish language that was still so new to her.

She had forgotten meeting Juan the first time, at a big party. He had remembered her. Was it because she stuck out so awkwardly from the crowd? When they were introduced the second time, Juan caught her to him, "Janet!" pronouncing the 'J' softly. He pulled her away from the others, and looked at her with keen brown eyes, with what she at first thought was a frown, but that might have been a question, and now she thought, even shortsightedness. Shortsighted about her! That was it! That made her giggle.

She was behaving peculiarly. Janet determined to pull herself, her real self, together, to be systematic about this whole affair. Affair! My God, what would her mother think of this? She would have to call, let her mother know that she wasn't coming to Ohio. Her mother always asked about old boyfriends, but they were, well, not at all like Juan. But what was he like? She hardly knew him and here she was, standing in a dark hotel room waiting for him to come in eight hours!

Janet pulled up a venetian blind. The window faced a grey-gold sea where waves broke into white petals and fell endlessly toward her, never reaching shore—like seconds, minutes, never to arrive at the 8 o'clock hour. Juan's twentieth hour, she reminded herself.

Too restless to stay in the room, Janet descended a wide flight of stairs and entered the mahogany-paneled dining room. The time was 11:40 a.m. The room was empty. She forced herself to read every item on the menu, then ordered a cup of coffee with cream. The waiter gave her a sly smile. She was a perfect setup for his game, a woman alone. Surely he thought she was waiting for someone, or a lover, and wasn't she?

"Anything else, Señorita? Isn't there something more you want?"

She stirred grains of sugar around in her cup. She never took sugar in her coffee, yet she had dumped in spoonfuls. She had to think. Let her rational mind take over, not rash behavior. Agreeing to meet Juan made her vulnerable. She felt the soft edges of her self-worth crumbling. Was he only interested in her because, like others, she had been taken by his charm?

When he wrote "Yours forever, Juan" did he mean the forever? He had taken her hand in a comic sort of handshake at the last party.

"Good-bye, Señorita Janet," he said. But when he turned away from her she felt alone. Her desire had taken form only as a sea swell, never breaking into the effulgence of the expected. No crashing waves, but in her heart there was a slow washing of desire—she was swimming toward an unknown shore.

Once before, when she had been at the airport, milling in the crowds, waiting for a flight to Miami and then Ohio, Juan had surprised her. He had put his arm around her and said, "El-o Janet." (She thought fleetingly he had practiced not to slur the 'J'.) "Janet!" he said again.

She met his mother and sisters there and a brother who was leaving on a flight. When introduced, the family smiled and made comments so rapidly, all talking at once, that she hadn't understood what they said and she hadn't been able to think of anything to say in Spanish – in fact, anything at all – except "I am pleased to meet you."

How stupid she must have seemed. The brother had said something about Juan, and his family laughed and Juan had looked warmly at her, assured that she hadn't understood all they were saying. He had promised to get in touch with her, and he had. And now again—at the last moment.

She searched her purse to be sure she had Juan's note. The

purse contained all her papers – her identification, passport, health certificate, and the canceled airline ticket, all attesting to the fact of her existence, her very real self, Janet – sitting in the dining room, waiting for Juan.

When her mother had asked if she wasn't interested in any of the old boyfriends, she had confessed that she was interested in someone, but she wasn't sure how interested he was in her. "Don't go getting yourself 'mixed up' with any foreigner, Janet. Marriage is hard enough, without all that extra."

"All that extra" was why Janet had to visit her father in Miami and her mother in Ohio.

From the window of her hotel room, Janet saw a park. Hoping to still her doubts and quicken the lagging hours, she crossed a wide boulevard separating the hotel from the park and strolled on a long walkway at the edge of the sea.

Children played on swings, and their shadows, by late afternoon, glanced back and forth across the grass, oblique silhouettes like moving cutouts. This was a magic hour and theirs a magic age. So impulsive, the children. And Juan also, like the child in her class, the one who wrote "Te Amo" three inches high in red crayon.

In the park, small boys chased squealing girls in pretty dresses, hugging them or tumbling them onto the grass. They cried, laughed, and quarreled, and filled buckets with sand in the hours between naptime and supper. Maids attended the children. Someone discovered almonds in a tree and children jumped for the almond pods nestling in branches. The children shouted, *"Deme, deme,* give me!"

They bit into the woody succulence, a sudden thirst quenched by the unexpected treat. Leaves and branches shredded last light of afternoon into ribbons that broke in golden patches in the grass. Janet had a momentary sense of well-being, a feeling that she was breaking away from a long childhood. But wasn't she, like a child, grabbing for something that did not belong to her?

Clouds gathered heavily on the horizon at the evening hour. Waves broke, rolled on endlessly, swelling in white froth on the shore. Janet felt the island of herself, until now contained, washing away. New seas were breaking over her and she didn't know where they were carrying her—and maybe she didn't care.

She wasn't Cinderella changed into a princess, sitting in the hotel lobby, she knew that. Plain and prim was how she looked, with her purse on her lap and Juan's note in it. She reread the letter. The effect had not changed. But would the pumpkin burst? The 8 o'clock hour had come and he wasn't here!

Then she was startled by a voice over her shoulder saying, "El-o, hello, Janet!"

She jumped up quickly, too quickly. He was there, touching her, holding her face in his hands, placing her face into the one he remembered and then her image of him cleared, became the one she saw before her.

"Then you are not leaving?"

"No," she said, "I'm not leaving."

~~~

That had been a long year ago and now Janet was at the airport waiting for her plane. But this time she would go. She had to have time to - surely she must - convince herself that she would return.

As she ran across the tarmac to her plane, Juan's voice pursued her. "Janet! Janet, I'm sorry!"
~~~

The Old Man

Pedro's *alpargatas*, his woven sandals, soles made from old tires, drag across the asphalt of Calle Zamuro. The sun seems to sulk, refusing to move across the sky, and the vermillion blossoms of flamboyant trees in the plaza lick flameward as if caught on fire from the sun's intensity.

He sits on a bench near the church, watching young boys roll a hoop or run sure-footed atop the ledge that separates the plaza from the road. Girls in school uniforms pass. Their black leather shoes shine. Who could pay for such shoes? And where are the girls with long braids? Girls have cut their hair and rolled it on plastic curlers. Chatter follows them, their white stockings pulled high on brown legs. They turn to those left behind and shout, *"Ciao!"*

Who says *"hasta luego,* until later" anymore? And what would he say—El General, Libertador de la Patria, what would he say?

Where were the young men to serenade their sweethearts in the evening? Now, blasts of transistor radios invade the plaza. When he was a boy, the mahogany doors of the church were open. Now they are closed and the narrow windows guard the interior from knowledge that vandals have stolen the reliquary.

La Loca flies toward him in her black mourning robes. "Old man," she says, "go home."

He does not understand.

"So you won't heed me, either?"

He can't find an answer.

Old Pedro is too tired to stand up. People move along Calle Zamuro, but he cannot distinguish one from another. Moisture wells in his dry eyes like pools of rain in sand. Then a terrible BOOM! His heart stops—was death upon him? Was it a cannon fired, or a firecracker?

With effort, he walks to the crossing where villagers gather in grey haze, bending low, shouting, shaking their heads. A few run from one side of the street to the other, looking, searching, for what? Pedro comes near—then wishes he had not seen the boy who was unable to get up, a flesh wound marking his leg.

Someone says, "It's Ana's boy!"

"Chico!"

"Ana, Ana, it's Chico!"

The mother, not comprehending, comes from her house, rubbing her hands against her thighs. She sees Chico.

"*Mi niño! Mi cariño!*" She runs to the boy, holds him in her arms. "My child! My dear one!"

"Ana, Ana, he will be all right! He bleeds, but the wound is not to the bone."

"What happened? What was it?"

"Like a bomb!"

"Yes, that is what it was!"

"A bomb!"

"The boy was just passing—strangers ran by."

"Perhaps an accident...?"

"It makes no sense!"

"I was standing here—heard it first before I knew what happened."

"A Molotov cocktail!"

"But why?"

"Same thing last week in Caracas."

"A bomb is not hard to make - a little kerosene - a bottle."

The boy sobs; the mother, relieved at this sign that life would continue, says, "Cariño, does it hurt much?"

"*Si, mucho*, Mama!"

The crowd lingers and the old man hears La Loca muttering to the wind, "Foolish people, evil ones, where will it end? Where will it end?"

As the dust and refuse swirl down Calle Zamuro, old Pedro sees that blood on the street already dries and soon will disappear from memory.

Cerveceria

Men come to the *cerveceria* as to a sacrament, to assemble at the table of declamation, slaking their thirst for manhood lost in a disinterested world. They raise glasses in ritual, tossing words into a vortex, each man scrambling verbally atop a pyramiding phraseology, each carrying the other along until, overburdened, their words climb no further. Ideas waver or stumble for lack of fact or emotion, or stretch into new meanings, origins forgotten, ideas carried toward a thought line, then punched down by hyperbole or tumbled apart in laughter, occasionally raised in anger or lingering in side whispers.

~~~

An old car, scarred by a history of bumps and battles, the rear door tied to the frame by a rope, a political *bandera* flapping from the window, rolls slowly down the highway. The driver, Eduardo, sits erect, playing freely with the wheel as the car in a slow glide finally arrives at the gasoline pump.

"Dios! We managed it!" says one of the men at the rear who had been pushing the vehicle. "This car is spoiled with such pampering."

"And I am a wreck!" says Oscar, wiping his face on his sleeve.

Olivo unbuttons the sweat-soaked front of his shirt. "*Hombres,*
~~~

we would be in better condition if Eduardo didn't own this car. If he hadn't had a rich uncle…" Olivo quickly crosses himself. "If we weren't celebrating that fact, I gladly would have driven my car."

Young Manuel, less winded than the others, looks hopefully toward the cerveceria.

Eduardo sticks his head out the car window. "How about loaning me a few *centavos* for gasoline?"

"Friend, we don't pay for a ride we don't get!"

"Walk then!" says Eduardo.

"*¡Dios mio!* Walking is easier than pushing this car!"

Eduardo gets out and sorts through his pockets.

The roadside bar and the gas station are part of a cluster of low buildings clinging together like dried seed pods outside the refinery gate. Villagers come by bus, others by car, refinery workers flocking to the cerveceria and the market where bottles of wine share shelves with rice, tomatoes, and black beans. At the rear of the market hangs a fresh carcass of goat, covered with flies. Squawking chickens dangle from a farmer's hand while villagers bargain a poor man's price. Trucks overloaded with bananas and oranges come from the mountains to the market.

The sun sets under mesquite trees as Oscar, Olivo, and Manuel enter the bar and see Salvatore, the fisherman, hunched there. Above him, a light bulb shines on the countertop, revealing old gouges under layers of varnish, scattered beer bottles, and discarded lottery tickets. A sign over the bar exclaims, "*Tome Cerveza! Cerveza Polar!*"

"Salvatore, how does it go with you, *pescadero?*"

"Not good."

"Doesn't the government set prices for your fish? My wife complains about the cost."

"What good are good prices when we don't catch fish?"

"Do the foreigners catch them all with their big nets?"

Salvatore stretches his head back and lets the last contents of a bottle slide down his throat. "I'm going out with them tomorrow."

"What? Giving up the *Pajaro?*"

"At least for a while."

"Then good luck, Salvatore!"

Oscar sits down at a table opposite the bar. "Does this table look good to you?" he asks.

"Same as always."

"Well, sit down, before somebody grabs it."

"I bet you grabbed it, Oscar, right out of the refinery yard."

The table is covered with stained oilcloth and sprinkled with cigarette ash. Oscar lifts a corner of the cloth. "Yes, the same table, for sure!"

"I don't see much of anyone else in here yet," says Manuel.

"Who are you expecting, Gloria?"

"Ah, Gloria," says Eduardo, "the dream *apasionado!*"

At the rear of the cerveceria a door opens and Manuel, in a moment of expectation, eyes caught in the glow of the light bulb, thinks it is Gloria. But it is Soledad, her mother, who comes out of the darkness like a priestess, sure in manner and gravity of expression, her black hair smoothed back from a large face, her figure broad, great gold earrings quivering as she leans over the table. With slight disdain in her voice, she says, "Don't you men ever wash?"

"We had a little job to do. Since the world turns slowly, we had to give Eduardo's car a push."

Soledad sets three bottles of cold Polar on the table.

"Where is Gloria?" asks Manuel.

"None of your business, handsome."

"But it is your business, isn't it, Soledad?" asks Oscar. Soledad ignores him. She is spare, with the containment of one who has outlasted her youth and is grateful. It is for her daughter, Gloria, that all men wait, eyes raised whenever the back door opens.

"But," says Olivo, "the high price of fish is right for you, eh, Salvatore, if everyone eats fish!"

"It depends on the fish," says Salvatore. "We fishermen don't go on strike as you do at the refinery. It is the fish that strike, don't bite. But for you men of the refinery the seas are not rough. You stub your foot on your lunch bucket and the boss comes over and shakes your hand and pays you a bonus. You throw up your hands and say, 'we don't like this or that,' so nobody works. We fishermen go out for the catch whether the price is up or down. I am the one who must live by luck, whether the fish bite or not."

"Because I have a job at the refinery, you cannot call that luck. But for you, Salvatore," says Olivo, "if the winds blow strong from the sea, then I am sorry."

"And tomorrow," asks Manuel enthusiastically, "you start with the gill-netters, the big ships?"

"But isn't it true, Salvatore," asks Olivo, "that the big fishing boats already have destroyed the shrimp beds off the coast and now must travel very far, in foreign waters?"

Salvatore nods, and without answering, sets the coin in his hand down hard on the counter and walks out of the cerveceria.

"Too bad that Salvatore can't take his own boat out anymore."

"That is what we call progress—bigger boats, bigger problems."

"Here's Eduardo marching in! Has the car expired, Eduardo?"

"The condition is somewhat delicate, but the machine with some gasoline should improve. A few coins from you and one small push, señores, and the car will be in good health!"

"Eduardo, I am no *medico* and I refuse to push that car one centimeter more."

"If you hadn't pushed, where would you be?"

"At home, without all these aches and pains!"

"You would be without your *compañeros*, your companions." Eduardo claps his hands and Soledad comes to the table with more beer.

The men watch thoughtfully as Dominico of the syndicate comes over, pulls a chair from the next table and straddles it, lights a cigarette, and watches the match burn. He waits a moment, staring at the end of his cigarette, then inhales deeply, slowly releasing the smoke through clenched teeth. He braces his arms on the chair back and stares at the men around the table. They are silent.

"*Compadres*," says Dominico. "My friends, did you see my sign?"

"What sign, Dominico?"

"Near the refinery gate. Some of my boys painted it last night. 'DOWN WITH THE IMPERIALISTS!' it says. How do you like that, in thirty-centimeter lettering?"

"Covering up old election signs?"

"This is just the beginning. You see those *ricos*, the rich ones going by out there in their big cars?"

Eyes stray to the doorway, to car lights passing on the highway.

"Those rich foreigners go by out there, rolling right over you. It is time," says Dominico, "for you to get up and say that some of that belongs to you!"

"But Eduardo here, just got a car. What can you say to capitalists like him?"

"To help him by pushing the car, that is my experience!" says Olivo.

"Olivo, the imperialist lover, would see us rot without jobs while he sits on a fat job at the refinery working for foreigners."

"And when did your talk, Dominico, ever make money for the people here?" Olivo, angered, rises from his chair. Eduardo grabs his arm to keep him down.

"Señores," says Dominico, "I work for the syndicate because of a sense of patriotism. I don't work for the foreigners. The syndicate works to give the people what by right is theirs."

"What do you mean, Dominico? You were not born here."

"Twenty years. All the years that count! Now I intend to kick the *imperialistas* out on their butts. What about that, Olivo? The syndicate is forcing the oil company to pay the foreigners off in order to get them to leave the country. And they are leaving, chasing after their dollars."

"Dominico," says Oscar, lowering his voice, "for the syndicate, do you need equipment? I am in the procurement business. Tables, chairs, almost anything."

Dominico crushes the butt of his cigarette in a glass and draws his chair closer to the men at the table. "A revolution will overthrow foreign intervention by the imperialists. It will be a revolution against capitalists."

Eduardo bangs his bottle on the table as an exclamation of dissent. Soledad thinks it is a call for more beer and brings another round to the table.

"Soldier, where are your compañeros this evening?" she asks a young soldier from the National Guard who has sauntered into their midst.

"Bring him a Polar, Soledad!"

The soldier, in fatigues, thumbs the gun in his belt.

"Hola, friend," says Eduardo. "What goes?"

"Haven't you heard?" asks the young soldier.

"Heard what?"

"About the *guerillas?* It's all over the radio."

"So when are guerillas news anymore?" says Dominico. "They are everywhere."

Eduardo pulls up a chair. "Sit down with us."

"You haven't heard?"

"No."

"Well, I was there!"

"Where?"

"Tell us!" says Eduardo. "Much happens that we do not hear."

"And much we hear doesn't happen!" says Olivo, pouring beer into a glass and sliding it across the table to the young *guardia*.

"Well, yesterday," he lowers his head as if he ought not be overheard, "our unit was called out. There was a report of guerillas near Rio Seco."

"Yes, go on!"

"The police had received a report of a plane circling there. A patrol encountered guerillas and one of the men got a bullet in the leg. After many shots were fired, the guerillas disappeared into the hills near the mountain. But the patrol swore that just as the sun was setting, they heard a plane take off."

"Was the plane carrying drugs? Guns?"

"How were they to know? They didn't capture anyone. So this morning, there we were, jumping off the trucks at the same spot. Imagine how it was, running from cactus to cactus, not knowing where the guerillas were, and surprising only a few iguanas! We ran across the desert, guns ready in case the guerillas started firing."

"And what happened?"

"Nothing! But later we did encounter something very significant."

"Yes? What?"

"Tracks. Made by a plane. Interesting information for the government, no? We assumed, then, that the guerillas were not far away. So we marched on—on guard, I must say, for I want to keep my skin as much as any of you! We were at a disadvantage, too, with the guerillas having fled to the mountain, fully able to observe us without being seen. We progressed silently across the sand and headed to the hills… but I can't go into details."

"No, tell us. Proceed!"

"We found a cache of arms!"

"Guns! Where?"

"Only by extreme cleverness did we find where they were hidden. If you have been there, around Rio Seco, you know where I mean—near the mountain, where the hills rise abruptly."

"Where did you find the arms?"

"In half the night you wouldn't guess! They were in the *bodega*, the only store in the settlement."

"Yes," says Oscar, "I know the place! A few boards only. Sells hardly anything."

"But," says the soldier, "a clever concealment of guns and explosives was found there. Hidden under a false shelf with the floor dug out beneath."

"But did you find the guerillas?"

"No, and we almost didn't find the arms. If my compañero had not reached behind the counter to admire the fine handle of an unusual machete, wondering if he might acquire it one way or another, he wouldn't have noticed the crack between the bottom shelf and the dirt floor. Carbines, Russian rifles, and American grenades… but we could find no indication where the guerillas might be. Furthermore," continues the soldier, "the proprietress of the bodega admitted she sold the guerillas hammocks, blankets, and other provisions, but she denies knowing anything about the arms cache under the counter."

"My theory," says Eduardo, "is that the nearby residents are the guerillas and fade into the landscape at daylight and into their proper lives."

"The woman is involved, of course," says Olivo. "She makes a good thing of selling blankets and everything else!"

"Here it is! I knew it!" A man at the bar tunes a transistor radio. "The commercial comes on right about now, just before the news broadcast. Listen now! Have you heard this?"

A moment of static and then a baritone voice sings a snappy tango.

"Yes, in Russia they drink *pivo* – some places they call it beer – but in our great country – los hombres drink Polar!"

"That's him! That's Federico!"

"Federico has a good voice."

"He has a big success, now, in Caracas!"

"Play it some more."

"It's finished!" The news comes on with a rapid staccato… "just announced capture… six men… near Rio Seco… unauthorized airfield… further evidence of arms smuggling network… originating in Cuba… governor of the state replies, 'a slight abnormality caused by a gang of wild excursionists.'"

"He makes them sound ridiculous instead of dangerous," says the soldier.

"Either they will go underground or they will come into the open, fighting."

"*Vaqueros*, cowboys!" says Olivo. "They are not likely to run into anything but cactus in the seat of their pants."

"It will be a revolution for social justice," says Dominico.

"No, Dominico. Is that social justice? Fighting one's countrymen?"

"The problem is, everybody wants the power."

"Power is money."

"If money flows," says Eduardo, "blood does not flow in the streets."

"Mao Tse-tung," says Dominico, "has said that social justice will be won, not by tears, but by blood."

Soledad exchanges empty bottles with full, extracting monies for the collection in her pocket.

"Well, who has got change?" asks Eduardo. "Manuel? Oscar? Nobody? I paid for the gas, but here is change for the soldier and me."

"I'll go half with the rest. You see how it is," says Olivo, "with money in the pocket one must pay; while Dominico here, complains, he doesn't pay. And where would my friends be without the benefits they receive from the oil company, eh, Dominico?"

"Handsome," asks Soledad, "you finished that electrician's course you were bragging about?"

"Manuel brag? That boy can hardly speak."

Manuel nods.

"So, can you fix a hot plate for me, out back?"

"Manuel can fix anything, can't you? Speak up!"

"Yes."

Lights from traffic on the highway turn darkness into shadowy forms of junked cars, storage shacks, cases of empty beer bottles. "Watch out for that packing crate, Manuel," advises Soledad.

An electric generator rivets into the night air, challenging the beat of cha-cha-cha from a radio. At the screened door, Soledad says, "I have to get back to the customers."

Manuel is startled by his sudden propulsion into what seems to him a Garden of Eden. He has dreamed of Gloria, even to the smell of her perfume de gardenia, which now threatens to make him swoon. He tells himself to keep a steady hand in order to be able to fix the hot plate. And if he appears calm, not too interested at first, he might get a chance to embrace Gloria, maybe even crush, crush, crush her like petals of a gardenia.

"Gloria?"

"Yes?"

The screened door creaks.

Soledad tries to wipe ashes from the moist oilcloth on the table.

"Soledad," asks Oscar, "what have you done with Manuel? Did he get lost out back with Gloria?"

"Ah, Gloria," says Eduardo.

"What a vision!" says Oscar. "All of her…"

"Shut up, sharp mouth!" says Soledad.

"I was only remarking how beautiful your daughter is."

Dominico rises unsteadily, taking out a cigarette, trying to light it.

"Leaving, Dominico?" asks Olivo. "Take your old revolution with you!"

Light bulbs in the cerveceria dim, focus blurs. Later, Soledad brings coffee made on the electric plate out back.

Oscar, Olivo, and Manuel stand near the gasoline station.

"One time more, push!" They strain against the car.

"Loosen the brake, Eduardo, the brake!"

"It is, it is!"

They push, the car coughs, then moves forward as the men hop in, laughing. They are off into the night – like their countrymen – determined to arrive, the destination always another kilometer down the highway.

In these colorful vignettes,
Ina (Yount) Whitlock draws from ten years
of living in Venezuela. She also resided
in Aruba, Australia, and Norway.
Ina grew up in Lincoln, Nebraska and,
for the last quarter century, has lived
on Vashon Island in the state of Washington.

CPSIA information can be obtained at www.ICGtesting.com
Printed in the USA
BVOW021616220911

271798BV00005B/1/P